The Essence of Flycasting

The Essence of Flycasting
by Mel Krieger

Foreword by A. J. McClane
Photographs by Ben Blackwell
Edited by Nelson Ishiyama

The Countryman Press
Woodstock, Vermont

**Library of Congress Cataloging-in-
Publication Data**

Krieger, Mel, 1928–
   The essence of flycasting / by Mel
Krieger ; foreword by A.J. McClane ;
photographs by Ben Blackwell ; edited by
Nelson Ishiyama.—1st Countryman
Press ed.
      p. cm.
   Originally published: San Francisco,
Calif. : Club Pacific, 1987.
   ISBN: 0-88150-505-6 (alk. paper)
   1. Fly casting. I. Ishiyama, Nelson. II.
   Title.
SH454.2 .K74 2001
799.1'24—dc21
                        00-065981

Illustrations by Michael Felber
Interior design by Mike Riedel and Ford
Scott Rollo
Cover design by Deborah Fillion
Cover photograph by Ben Blackwell

Published by
The Countryman Press,
P.O. Box 748, Woodstock, Vermont 05091

Distributed by
W. W. Norton & Company, Inc.,
500 Fifth Avenue, New York, NY 10110

Printed in the United States of America

10 9 8 7 6 5 4 3 2 1

To my students, my mentors and my friends, many of whom have filled all of these roles. To my great kids, Sharon and Jan, and especially to my partner,

Fanny

Acknowledgments

To two talented friends whose time and efforts on this book more than equaled my own. Thank you Ben Blackwell and Nelson Ishiyama. This book is ours.

I also wish to thank A.J. McClane for his generous foreword. Additionally Karel Bauer, Ford Scott Rollo, Michael Felber, Mike Riedel and Mary Smiley.   □

Contents

Preface to the Countryman Press Edition

Both of us were intimidated. Ruth, a tiny, sixtyish woman, was taking my fly-fishing course in Sun Valley, Idaho, and while her big concern was learning to fly-cast, I would be attempting to teach one of the foremost educators in America. Both of us survived, actually becoming friends, but I didn't come out completely unscathed. During a lecture, one of the students, a compulsive note taker, persisted in asking, almost demanding, specific answers to his questions. "But, Mel, what is the exact length of a dry fly tippet? How many casts do I make to a fish before changing my fly? Are green waders less visible than brown ones?" After several interruptions and reasonably patient replies, I lost it. "Pete," I said, "you keep looking for black and white in fishing, and there is precious little black and white. The beauty of our sport is that it's more of an art form than a science. We are not dealing in absolutes. There are no absolutes!" I was on a roll. Voice rising, I proclaimed "There are no absolutes in fishing! There are no absolutes in casting . . . Damn it, there are no absolutes in life!!!" Silence filled the room. Embarrassed, I finally spotted her amid the quieted faces and blurted "Isn't that so, Ruth?" Loud and clear she replied "Absolutely!"

There is, however, one absolute in casting that must be stated. The secret of learning to flycast does not exist in the following pages, nor in other books and videos or in the words and pictures of any instructor. The only way to learn flycasting is to flycast! This, above all, is the essence of the learning experience. The quintessence of learning is doing!

Instruction merely provides avenues for learners. Many instructors utilize a very narrow corridor, teaching an extremely concise style that can be comfortable for some beginners. Wider corridors usually emphasize more substance than style, offering a somewhat broader base for growth, generally useful to a larger number and variety of learners. Most instruction in flycasting and in other physical disciplines such as tennis or golf consists of analysis. Some instructors become quite good at analyzing the flycasting stroke or the golf swing, a skill that is primarily useful to the advanced learner. There are fewer gifted instructors who understand many styles, and who can analyze the student as well as the casting stroke or the golf swing, fitting one to the other without the loss of fluidity and athleticism. Fewer still are the instructors who are also good communicators, able to reduce complex concepts to simpler solutions and to reach and connect with a wide variety of learners. Simplicity is not an easy concept—it is perhaps the most difficult part of instruction. I must tell you of my own experience.

Nelson Ishiyama, a friend and the editor of this book, did more than help me with words. Early in our work together, he asked me if the purpose of the book was to teach people to cast. The real truth was that I wanted to show my peers and the world that once and for all, the fly cast would be completely and perfectly analyzed, and that it would be carved in stone forever and ever, and that Mel Krieger would be recognized as the author of flycasting's theory of relativity. Somehow I had trouble admitting this, even to myself—so I agreed to adopt the "will this help someone learn to cast?" approach to everything we did in this book.

We spent a lot of time attempting to reduce complicated and involved theoretical concepts to more basic truths and to simpler explanations. We eliminated hundreds of photos and illustrations, and many, many words. We hope this simplification will bring us closer to the essence of flycasting.

Beyond all of this, there exists those ultimate teachers, those extraordinary and wondrous people who are able to go beyond simple explanation to inspire students to want to learn, to grow, to understand that the climb is even more exciting than the summit, and who, themselves, continue to learn and to grow. To me—the quintessence of teaching is inspiration!

If somehow, through the words and pictures in this little manual, I can convince you of that concept, the true pleasure of flycasting will be yours. New friend, I wish you this.

Introduction

I'm sure that most of you wish this book would instantly transform you into an accomplished flycaster and fisher. If somehow it could, you would miss one of the most exciting and enjoyable experiences in our sport, because the learning can be even more rewarding than the mastery. Flycasting offers a lifetime of delightful learning experiences. I envy those of you who are beginning, and I respect all of you who continue to learn.

Learning to cast a fly is fun, each plateau fueling an eagerness for the next. Although the discoveries of the newcomer may be more dramatic, breakthroughs in flycasting aren't just for beginners. I was reminded of this on a recent trip with a good friend in Argentina. At 68, Jorge Donovan, an expert caster and internationally known flyfisher, is a man of strong convictions. He can also be stubborn. For years he resisted those special lines called shooting tapers, until one day not long ago. A stiff breeze blew off the pampas as our small group fished a large river with nymphs and streamers. Although some of the group were inexperienced casters, they all covered the water well, using shooting tapers to make easy 70-foot casts. We stopped for lunch on a long gravel bar, and while the rest of us were eating, Jorge, who had watched in silence all morning, picked up my rod and began casting. After several frustrating minutes, he developed the feel of the new line and began to cast well, each cast a little farther than the previous one. Soon he was belting out casts of well over 100 feet. I walked over and asked what he thought of my outfit. "Not bad," he said calmly as he stripped even more line from the reel. Then, losing all of his impressive composure, he straightened up and started to giggle, finally laughing loudly with the sheer delight of his new discovery.

This book alone will not make you a flycaster. The only way to learn flycasting is to experience it, to teach *yourself* to cast a fly. Instruction can only encourage and guide you in this learning process. Most of you who are developing a flycasting stroke will need 10 to 20 hours of practice to become reasonably proficient and to control the line and fly well enough to fish comfortably. It's a stage similar to the point in tennis when you spend more time playing points than picking up the balls.

The instruction in this book is designed to progress from basic to advanced flycasting and fly presentation. Although each chapter attempts to treat a subject completely, most depend to some extent on information in preceding chapters. I recommend that you first read the book in its entirety, and only then work on the various casting techniques. I have tried to emphasize the *essence* of flycasting—concepts that apply to proficient casters as well as beginners. I wish you well.

You will know something of me after reading this book. I hope that on some fine trout stream our paths will cross, and I will get to know you. □

1

The Mechanics of Flycasting

Before we start to cast a fly, it is useful to understand some of the mechanics—the "whys"—of a flycast and what it is you hope to achieve. All accomplished casters, regardless of their styles, utilize the same basic mechanics to make a good cast. If you have difficulty relating to some of the more technical information, don't be concerned. Just read through it and look at the illustrations. After you practice the various casts, the information in this chapter will be easy to understand. Keep the book handy, and reread this chapter as you try the exercises.

Almost all other casting techniques employ a compact weight that is hurled through the air, pulling a light line behind it. Flycasting permits us to present a weightless lure by using the weight of the line. It would be natural to assume that a heavy fly would work best. Fortunately that's not true. In fact, the lighter the fly, the easier it is to cast with a fly rod. One of the wonders of the sport is casting a virtually weightless fly—a wisp of a feather—20, 30, 50 feet and presenting it as delicately as a mosquito dropping to the water.

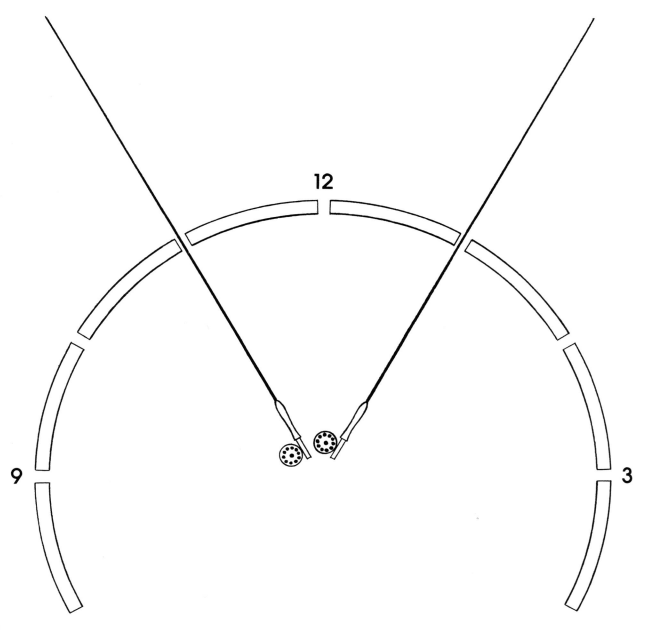

The weighted line, like a long whip, must be cast backward and forward. I believe it was Jim Green, a noted rod designer and caster, who first described flycasting as rolling a line back and forth in the air. We create this rolling motion by *slinging* the line through the air, stopping the rod and allowing the line to unroll off the tip of the rod. This entire motion—from start to stop—is called the CASTING STROKE. The V-shaped arc between the rod in the start position and the rod in the stop position is called the CASTING ARC. The shape of the line as it unrolls through the air is called the CASTING LOOP.

In explaining a basic casting stroke to flycasting students, instructors often use different positions on a clock face to indicate relative positions in a casting arc. For example, instructors typically use the phrases "eleven o'clock to one o'clock" or "ten o'clock to two o'clock" to describe the V-shaped casting arc. Such fixed casting arcs can be useful tools in the initial education of a flycaster because they provide a consistent form for learning timing, power application and the basic feel of casting. Unfortunately, most instruction stops at this point, and many flyfishers spend a lifetime erroneously trying to stop their backcast at twelve o'clock or one o'clock or wherever. Instruction limited to any of these fixed casting arcs is incomplete. Good flycasting and fishing are based on variations in both the position and the size of the casting arc.

Eleven o'clock to one o'clock is *just one of the many casting strokes (arcs) you need.*

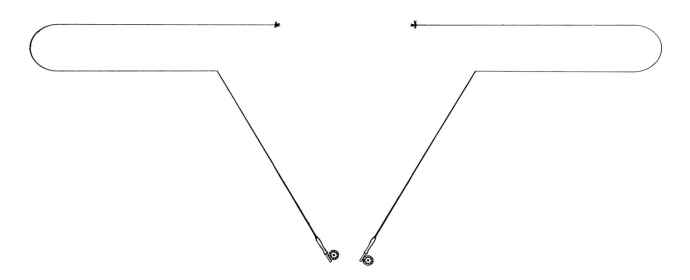

Parallel cast— upright casting arc

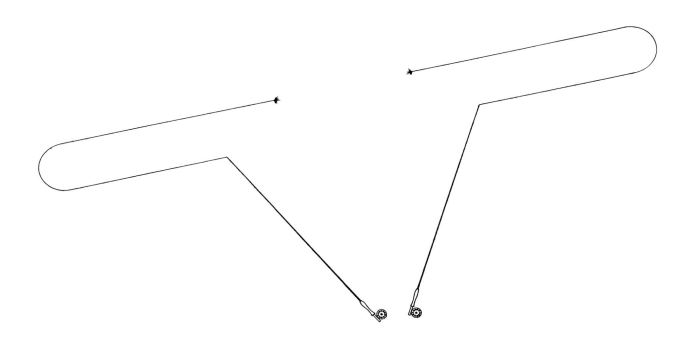

High forward cast—casting arc tilted back

The Position of the Casting Arc

Good flycasting requires that the backcast and the forward cast work together in a straight line. The direction of that line determines the position of the casting arc. For example, a cast parallel to the water (front and back) requires an upright casting arc (e.g., eleven o'clock to one o'clock or ten o'clock to two o'clock). The entire casting arc must be tilted backward to get a higher forward cast or tilted forward to get a higher backcast. Varying the position of the casting arc isn't difficult to learn and is obviously a requisite to good casting and fishing.

*Vary the **position of the casting arc** to change the angle of the cast.*

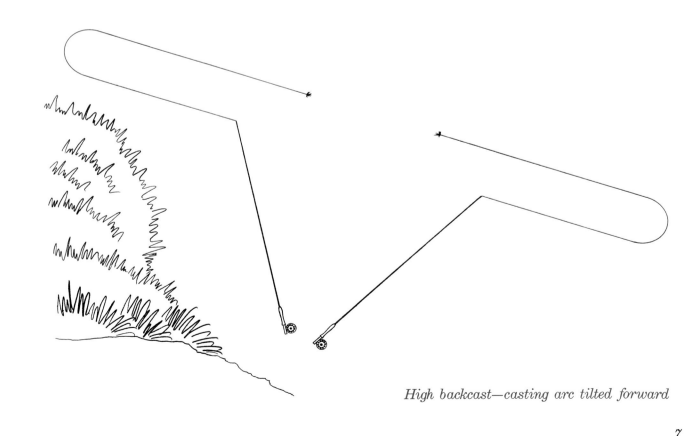

High backcast—casting arc tilted forward

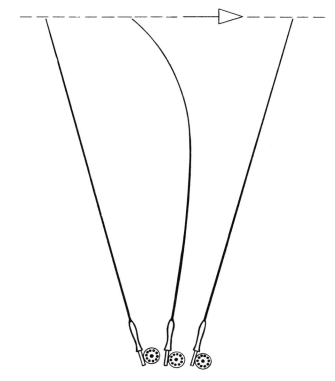

Minimal rod bend—narrow casting arc

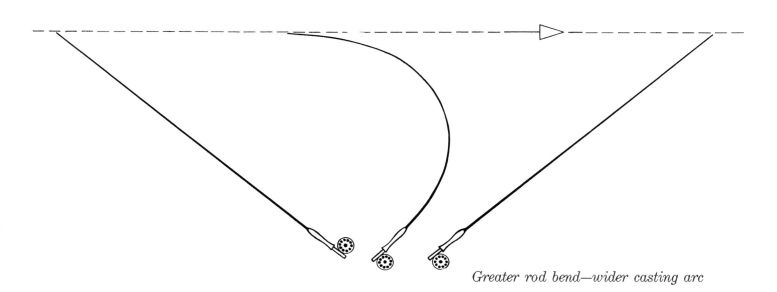

Greater rod bend—wider casting arc

The Size of the Casting Stroke, or Arc

Flycasting requires casting strokes (arcs) of all sizes. In order to keep the rod tip in a straight-line path (a necessity, as you will soon see), you must adjust the size of the casting arc to fit the amount of bend in the rod. The amount of bend in the fly rod is determined by: 1) the amount of weight (fly line) you cast, 2) the amount of power you apply, and 3) the stiffness of the fly rod. The greater the bend in the rod, the longer the casting stroke must be to maintain the straight-line path of the rod tip. Matching the amount of power you apply (which determines rod bend) with the casting arc size is one of the keys to good flycasting. That translates into a narrow stroke for short casts and a wider stroke for long casts. You will pick this up very naturally. The only danger is in limiting yourself to a restricted casting stroke.

*To maintain the straight-line path of the rod tip, adjust the **size of the casting arc** to match the amount of the bend in the rod.*

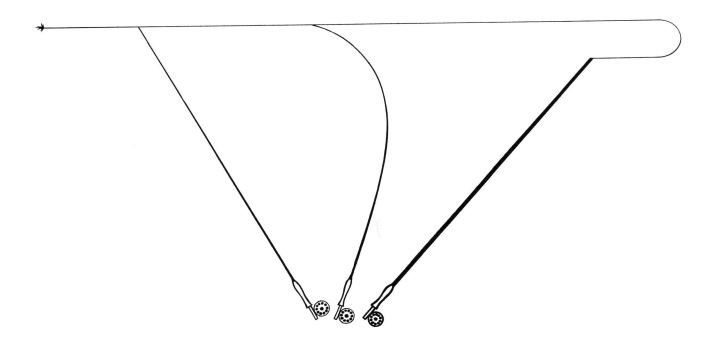

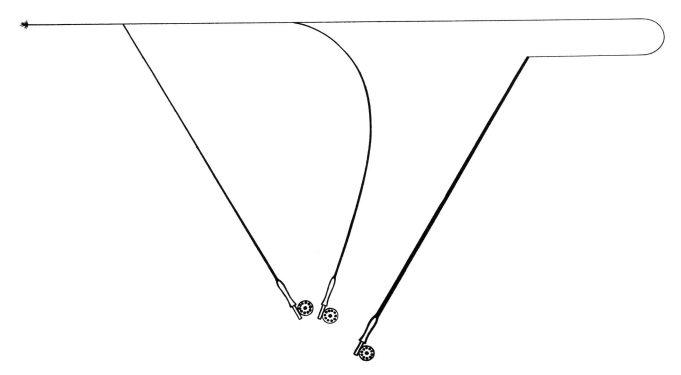

Forming the Casting Loop

A good casting loop is formed by decisively stopping the rod at the end of the casting stroke. When the rod tip stops, the line that has been following continues to fly forward; the stopped rod tip serves as an anchor point for the moving fly line, and a casting loop forms. The casting stroke must always conclude with the rod tip below the path of the line in the air, so that the line can pass over the rod tip rather than collide with it. You accomplish this by tipping the rod down slightly at the end of the casting stroke or by pulling the hand and rod tip down at the end of the stroke.

*Stopping the rod in this **tilted-forward position** allows the line to pass over the rod tip and form a casting loop.*

Pulling the rod down *as the casting stroke concludes also allows the line to pass over the rod tip and form a casting loop.*

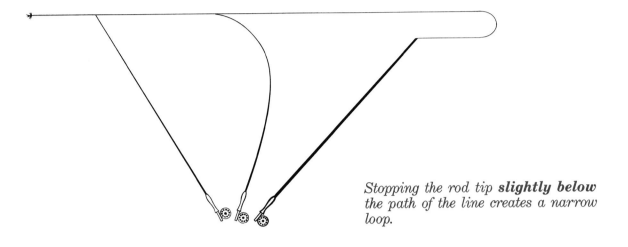

*Stopping the rod tip **slightly below** the path of the line creates a narrow loop.*

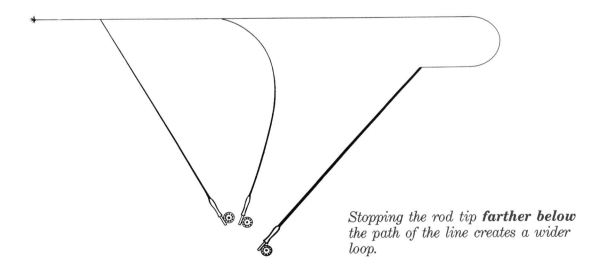

*Stopping the rod tip **farther below** the path of the line creates a wider loop.*

The Size of the Casting Loop

The position of the rod tip at the conclusion of the casting stroke controls the size of the casting loop. Generally, stopping the rod tip slightly below the path of the fly line as the casting stroke concludes results in a narrow loop, while stopping the rod tip farther below the path of the fly line as the casting stroke concludes causes a wider loop. Narrow loops are generally more efficient than wider loops simply because they encounter less air resistance. The resulting increase in line speed produces greater control and distance in flycasting. Some situations call for a wider loop. Use one, for example, if you are casting a long, delicate leader that has a tendency to fall back on itself.

The concept that narrow casting strokes produce narrow loops and that wide casting strokes produce wide loops is incorrect. By correctly applying power to the rod, you can make narrow or wide loops with *both* narrow and wide casting strokes.

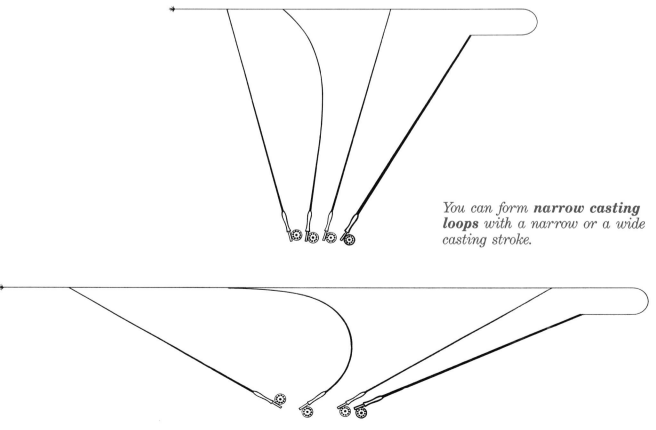

*You can form **narrow casting loops** with a narrow or a wide casting stroke.*

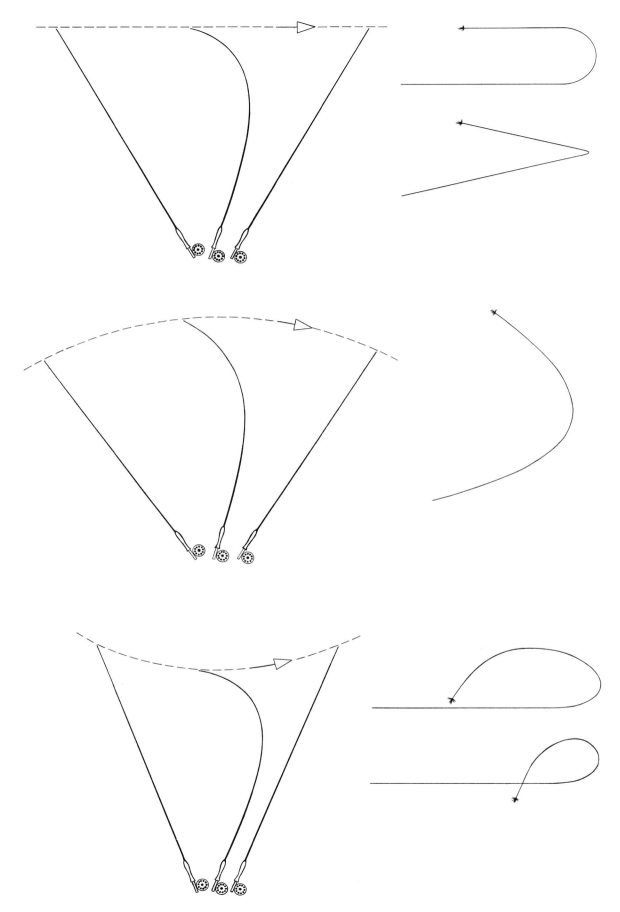

The Shape of the Casting Loop

The path of the rod tip during the casting stroke determines the shape of the casting loop; a straight-line path results in good loops; a convex path produces open loops, or non-loops. A concave path of the rod tip or fly line will cause tailing or crossed loops.

The best casting loops look like a tipped over U or V. As the most efficient loop shapes, they permit maximum distance and optimum control of the fly line and fly. Good loops result from a correct blend of rod bend and casting arc size and from an even and continuous application of power during the casting stroke, both of which produce the straight-line path of the rod tip.

Non-loops, also called open loops, are the least efficient and frequently cause the line to collapse in a pile. Such very large or non-loops are formed by a convex path of the rod tip as power is applied to the line. Open loops usually develop because a caster fails to load (bend) the rod adequately and/or uses too large a casting arc. This kind of "roundhouse" swing is common with beginners.

Tailing loops, in which the line crosses or hits itself while unrolling, cause tangled or knotted leaders (called wind or casting knots) and are considerably less efficient than good loops in terms of line control and distance. They are most often caused by too narrow a casting arc, or by an erratic or too-early application of power, which causes the rod tip to dip (concave path of the rod tip or fly line) during the casting stroke. This particular poor loop shape often plagues intermediate and even many experienced casters.

After taking you through this somewhat technical explanation, I want to reassure you that casting a fly is essentially a very simple discipline. These mechanics are for those of you who have to know "why" and to give all of you an overview of this gentle sport. Almost all experienced flycasters develop the timing and feel of good flycasting by rolling the line back and forth in the air a number of times. Together, the rhythm and the wonderful feel of the rod loading and slinging the line make up the essence of flycasting. □

*A **straight-line path** of the rod tip results in excellent U- or V-shaped loops.*

*Swinging the rod tip in a **convex path** produces very wide or non-loops.*

*A **concave path** of the rod tip causes tailing or crossed loops.*

2

Equipment

Fly Rod

The beginning flyfisher should purchase a fly rod about 8 1/2 or 9 feet long to balance with a 6- or a 7-weight line. Most rods have the appropriate line weight written on them. This is an excellent all-around size for freshwater fishing in most areas, but any fly rod size that suits your particular fishing interest will also work well as a practice rod. Although fly rods made of fiberglass and bamboo can perform well, I believe the modern rods of lightweight graphite are superior casting and fishing tools.

Fly Reel

You should have a single-action reel large enough to hold approximately 100 yards of 20-pound test braided dacron backing in addition to a full floating fly line. The 100 yards of backing has the effect of enlarging the diameter of the spool, resulting in a faster line retrieve and preventing the fly line from being stored in small kinky loops. (And when you hook Moby Trout, you will need all that backing for his long runs.) You also need an extra spool for your reel.

Fly Lines

Start with a good quality weight forward floating fly line. I prefer a light colored line for both fishing and practice simply because it's easier to see.

Purchase a medium sinking shooting taper (an outstanding training line) for your extra

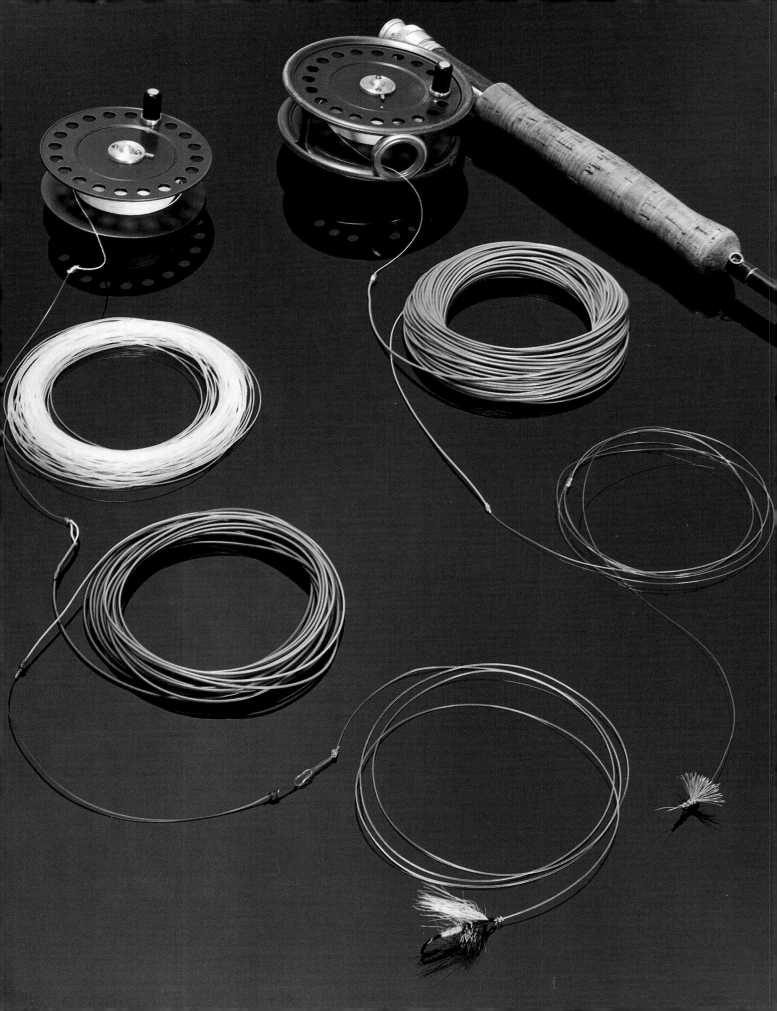

spool. Casting with this denser, smaller-diameter line will familiarize you with the faster timing needed for sinking fly lines. This 30-foot fly line should be one size larger than your floating line (e.g., a fly rod that balances with a 6-weight floating line requires a 7-weight shooting taper). The increased weight makes it easier to get the maximum load (bend) in the rod, which is required for distance casting. You will also need 100 feet of brightly colored monofilament (20- or 25-pound test) in addition to backing. Use enough backing to effectively fill up the extra spool.

Leaders

You will need a tapered leader 6 to 9 feet long with a tip strength of about 6 or 8 pounds. Attach 1 inch of brightly colored yarn as a practice fly. The leader is a necessary part of the fly line. Do not cast without it, as the fly line will not roll out correctly and you will damage the fly line.

General Rod/Line Table

Fly lines are numbered according to the weight of their first 30 feet and balanced with rods of corresponding stiffness. The following table provides general guidelines on the kinds of fishing done with various matched lines and rods.

Equipment you must have includes: (right) single action reel, backing, weight forward floating line and leader; (left) an extra reel spool with backing, 100 feet of monofilament running line, 30-foot sinking shooting taper and leader.

Line Weights	Line Types	Flies	Fishing
2 and 3	floating	delicate dry flies and nymphs	light trout
4 and 5	floating	small dry flies, wet flies and nymphs	light trout, panfish
6 and 7	floating, sinking	dry flies, wet flies, nymphs; small bass bugs, hair bugs and streamer flies	general purpose trout; light black bass, light steelhead and salmon, light bonefish
8 and 9	floating, sinking	large flies and bass bugs	heavy duty trout, general purpose black bass, steelhead and salmon, bonefish; light saltwater fish
10 and 11	floating, sinking	large flies	heavy duty salmon and steelhead; general purpose saltwater
12, 13, 14, 15	floating, sinking	very large flies	tarpon, sailfish, heavy duty saltwater

3

Form in Flycasting

The most significant help—other than encouragement and inspiration—that instruction can offer to a developing flycaster may well be good casting form. Almost everyone who persists in slinging a fly line back and forth learns to cast fairly well. Unfortunately, many people develop awkward styles that are often limiting, fatiguing and a handicap to further progress in flycasting and fishing. Better form at the outset makes learning easier and results in a more natural and comfortable casting stroke. Take the time to practice these hand and arm positions. You don't even need equipment. Use pantomime movements to develop this cornerstone of flycasting. The instruction in this book assumes a right-handed caster. My apologies to the "lefties" of the world.

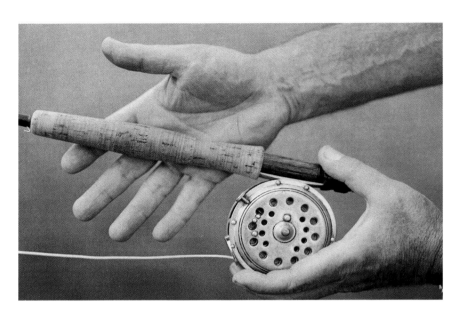

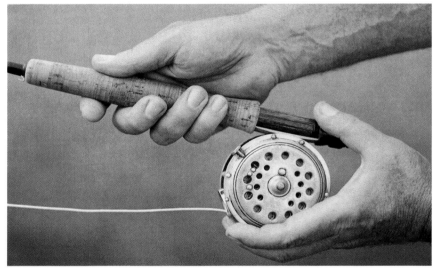

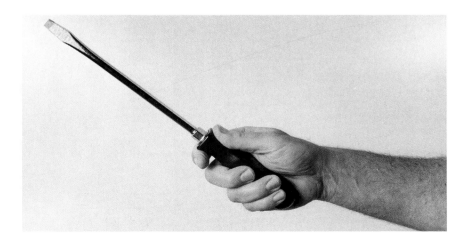

Grip

Good casting form begins with a correct grip. The infinitely adaptive human hand has grasped a straight fly rod handle in every conceivable manner. Although great flycasters and fishers have used every imaginable grip to good effect, there is one handhold that is superior to all others: the EXTENDED FINGER GRIP. This extremely comfortable, versatile hand position combines some of the best attributes of all the other grips. It is the strongest possible hand position for flycasting, offers superb control and lends itself perfectly to the numerous variations in modern flycasting strokes. A large percentage of today's better flycasters use some form of this grip, which strongly resembles the right hand grip in golf and the handshake grip in tennis. It is also like the hand position used to hold a screwdriver or a cooking whisk.

Start with your thumb on top of the handle and your last three fingers slanting down the handle toward your wrist. Your forefinger should extend well up the handle so that the second joint of your forefinger is about even with the end of your thumb. Hold the handle toward the end of your fingers rather than in your palm. Keep your wrist and hand reasonably straight so that the bottom of the fly rod extends out a few inches from your wrist. Take a fly rod or even a pen or pencil and spend some time getting familiar with this grip. Do it right now, as you read through these descriptions of good form in flycasting.

Move your hand and arm as if you were casting. Don't restrict yourself. Try rotating your hand (and the rod with it) so that your thumb is not always on top of the handle. Get comfortable. Notice how easy it is to tilt the rod to one side or the other as you rotate your hand and forearm. These canted rod positions are an integral part of flycasting.

Many good casters and fishers also rotate their casting hands to use variations of the

*To make the **Extended Finger Grip**, angle the rod handle from the middle joint of your forefinger to the fleshy pad at the heel of your hand.*

Grasp the handle with thumb on top and forefinger extended to a point opposite the end of your thumb. In casting with a firm wrist, the end of the rod should move no farther from your arm than shown here.

*You already use the **Extended Finger Grip** to hold a screwdriver.*

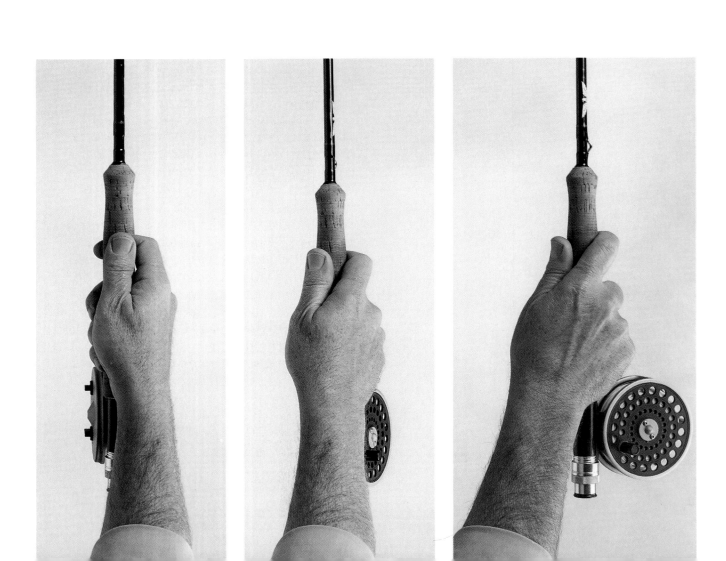

Extended Finger Grip for different casting situations. It is certainly reasonable to use a different hand position for a 10-foot dry fly cast than for an 80-foot steelhead or salmon presentation. Diversified hand positions also help reduce fatigue. I've put names on a few variations of the Extended Finger Grip. As you try these grips, just rotate the rod along with your hand rather than shifting your hold on the rod.

The basic Extended Finger Grip has the thumb directly on top of the handle. This grip offers excellent control and accuracy, especially for short casts, when your hand stays close to your body. It is also one of the strongest possible grips for backcasts.

A slight counterclockwise rotation of your hand results in the V GRIP. This grip has the thumb slightly to the left of the top of the handle. The base of the forefinger and the thumb form a V pointing toward your chin; they share in applying power on the forward cast. The V Grip variation is a very natural and comfortable hand position in a wide variety of casting strokes. I find myself using it most of the time.

A further counterclockwise rotation of your hand brings you to the PALM OUT GRIP. This grip has your thumb farther to the inside of the handle and the palm of your hand facing out toward the forward cast. (Note the angle of the reel in the V Grip and the Palm Out Grip photographs.) It is often used on long casts, when more power and a longer stroke are needed. On the forward cast, the base of the forefinger and the back of the hand supply more of the power than the thumb.

An experienced flycaster often uses two different grips during a cast by rotating his hand between the back and forward casts. On a long cast, for example, the Extended Finger Grip with the thumb on top gives maximum backcast strength, and the V Grip or the Palm Out Grip provides additional strength and an easier turnover of the rod tip in the forward cast. These grip variations are also commonly used to achieve the different planes that are needed in good flycasting. For example, off-shoulder casts (made on the left side of your

Left:

*From a caster's-eye view, the **Extended Finger Grip** has the thumb on top of the handle and the reel in a vertical plane.*

Center:

*Rotating the hand counterclockwise to the **V Grip** causes the reel to tilt slightly to the outside of the hand.*

Right:

*Greater counterclockwise rotation to the **Palm Out Grip** swings the reel farther to the outside of the hand.*

Left:

*With the **Extended Finger Grip,** the rod is upright and the reel is in a vertical plane.*

Right:

***Rotating the hand** counter-clockwise allows you to tilt the rod to the left while the forearm remains in a normal upright position. The reel is now tipped far to the outside of the hand.*

Left:

*Good **hand and arm position** for short casts and **short strokes** has the hand comfortably close to the shoulder and in front of the body at about chin height.*

Center:

*For longer casts and **longer strokes,** hand and arm must move higher and out from the shoulder.*

Right:

*For **longest strokes** and distance casts, the hand reaches farther up and out from the shoulder for maximum power.*

body and described in Chapters 4 and 5) require a rod angled to your left. Slightly rotating your casting hand is the easiest way to tilt the rod for these different angles.

Most fly rod handles are long enough so that you have a choice of grip placement. Placing your hand near the top of the fly rod handle and bracing the reel seat against your forearm provides excellent leverage when striking and playing large fish or picking up a long line. Personally, I prefer to position my hand at the bottom of the handle, close to the reel, when I cast. This grip placement seems to minimize the weight of the reel and to offer a better sense of "oneness" between my rod and hand. Use whatever is most comfortable for you.

Hand and Arm Position

Just as no single casting stroke encompasses the full range of flycasting and fishing situations, no fixed position for the hand and arm serves well for all conditions. The key to good position in all casting strokes is comfort. Start with your casting hand in front of your body and relatively close to your shoulder. Try to keep your elbow slightly forward of your body. For short casts, which usually require a short casting stroke, keep your hand only about as high as your chin and quite close to your shoulder. Get your hand up right now (without a rod or reel) and cast with me. The motion is something like hammering a nail in the wall in front of you. It's a bit more like throwing darts than pitching a baseball. Longer casts, with more line and a longer casting stroke, require an extension of your hand and arm both up and out from your shoulder. As the length of your casting stroke continues to increase (usually as you make longer casts), allow your hand to swing farther up and out until you reach an optimum throwing motion. Now you can throw that baseball.

As a general rule, make every effort to keep your hand as close to your shoulder as possible without distorting a comfortable throwing motion. This closer-to-the-shoulder hand position is much more comfortable and less fatiguing than the roundhouse baseball throw, which should be saved for extreme casting situations.

Foot Position

The correct stance is . . . all of them. It would be silly to limit yourself to one stance for the wide variety of fishing and casting situations. I recommend a squared stance for most of your practice, but spend some time with your right foot back. Offsetting your feet this way permits a longer casting stroke and allows you to watch your backcast or your rod or hand position. Do not get in the habit of watching every backcast, however. You may develop an awkward across-the-body casting stroke, miss something on the water in front of you and will probably wind up with "tennis neck." Also include some practice with the right foot forward, as this is an excellent position for accuracy. Once again, revert to the squared stance for most of your practice.

The Wrist in Flycasting

Although it is quite possible to cast well with full wrist movement, I strongly advocate keeping a very firm wrist. A firm wrist offers more control of the casting stroke and a quicker route to that special feel that is good flycasting. Even more important, it provides an easier and more efficient transfer of energy from your body to the fly rod. A floppy wrist is difficult to control and is probably the most common source of poor casting for beginning flycasters. A firm, controlled wrist is the one discipline in good form that at first may not feel completely natural. I suggest that you practice with a very firm wrist—think of it as almost rigid. Think of your forearm as a part of the rod. Think of casting with your forearm rather than your hand. Drop your right foot back and watch your casting hand as you cast. Most people have a small amount of wrist movement even when they think their wrist is completely stiff. As you develop the sweet feel of loading the rod and slinging the line, a limited wrist movement may even be desirable. It won't be long before a firm, controlled wrist becomes a natural and comfortable part of your casting stroke.

*A **stance** with your right foot back allows you to watch the backcast or your casting hand.*

Summing Up

I know that all of these words and pictures may appear complicated. Although single fixed positions in flycasting might seem easier to learn, the opposite is true. Fixed positions and concepts are, by definition, limiting. Variations in form are actually natural adaptations that might be likened to using short steps as you walk slowly and longer steps as you walk faster.

Learning, however, can begin on a simple note. Start with the Extended Finger Grip, and try to keep your hand somewhat in front of you and close to your shoulder. Allow yourself to move around. Try to find natural and comfortable positions for your arm and hand using the various flycasting strokes. I urge you to practice good form without rod or line. Pantomime practice develops muscle memory without the obvious distractions of actual flycasting.

Good form is also a totality, a coordinated effort by hands and arms and feet. You might even try bending your knees a little. Strive for a comfortable wholeness. Try to be graceful. □

Good form *is a relaxed and natural position of hands, arms and feet.*

4

The Roll Cast

The roll cast is a method of flycasting in which the line is rolled forward without a backcast. We use this cast to present a fly when obstacles, like trees or rocks or even a very strong following wind, prevent a normal backcast. We also use it to position the line prior to a pick up (e.g., roll casting a slack line into a straight position, roll casting a sunken line to the surface of the water or even changing the direction of the line on the water before picking it up).

The roll cast plays an important role in flycasting and fishing. Unfortunately, many instructors consider the roll cast of secondary importance, recommending it only for very short casts when a normal presentation is impossible. Recently I've become aware of how often I use it in an average day of fishing, even in situations where I can make a normal cast. Last year, fishing a small canyon stream in Idaho, I found myself choosing the roll cast to flick 10- or 15-foot casts into all the little nooks and crannies where fish lay. My fly was hardly ever out of the water, and I didn't have to bother with a backcast. Many times on big steelhead and salmon rivers in strong following winds, I have chosen the long roll cast because I didn't want to muscle backcasts into the wind all day. The roll cast is a winner and it is also a superb cast to begin the development of a good flycasting stroke. A few hours of practice with this very basic flycast goes a long way in teaching the casting form and power application that you use in all flycasts.

The roll cast is best done on water because you need some resistance on the front end of the line. Find a lake, pond, slow moving river or even a swimming pool where you can practice with 25 to 30 feet of line. If such a spot isn't readily available, a well watered lawn will do. Even a dry lawn can work if you use a little longer line—roughly 35 to 40 feet.

Work out about 25 or 30 feet of fly line to start this practice. The best way to do that is to place the leader and a few feet of line in the water in front of you and shake the needed line off the end of the rod. Notice that a locked wrist is a real help in shaking out line. Once you have the right amount of line out, hold the line coming from the reel against the rod handle with the middle finger (or forefinger) of your casting hand. Securing the line in this manner anchors the fly line while you cast and is essential to controlling the line while you fish. Do not hold the fly line with your left hand during this practice. Beginning casters often develop slack in the fly line between their line (left) hand and the fly rod.

Clamp the line against the rod handle with your middle finger or forefinger to practice the roll cast.

*Begin the **roll cast** by slowly bringing the rod to about one o'clock, keeping the end of the line in water in front of you. Allow the line to droop behind the rod. Your hand should be as high as the top of your head.*

Pull down and thrust forward to force a bend in the rod. You can see and feel that the sharply bent rod is part of the roll cast loop.

Stop the rod forcefully to transmit the power to the line. A powerful stop has caused the rod to bend sharply downward at the end of the stroke.

Driving forward, the elliptical loop rolls the line low over the water.

Although the rolling line disturbs the water close to you, it can deliver the leader and fly softly when it extends fully.

Lift the rod slowly to about the one-o'clock position, sliding the line in the water toward you. Your casting hand should be fairly high— about as high as the top of your head. Raising your hand lifts more line out of the water and creates a larger loop of line behind the rod. This improved line position and the longer casting stroke that results from the raised hand position permits a longer, easier roll cast. Tilt the rod away from your body so that the line hanging down from the rod tip falls freely to the outside of the rod. Be sure to bring the line back slowly, for the end of the line and leader must stay in the water in front of you. Wait until the line hanging from the rod tip falls slightly behind the rod tip. Pull the rod down and over (forward), aiming the cast slightly to the left of the line in the water in front of you. The line should roll out in the shape of an ellipse and present the fly.

The roll cast requires a bit more power than other casts, because you must load (bend) the rod without the pull of an airborne line. Imagine rolling a loop through the fly rod and into the line. A very firm wrist will be of real

At the beginning of the roll cast, tip the rod, swinging the line to the outside of the rod. To avoid tangles, cast to the left of the line in the water.

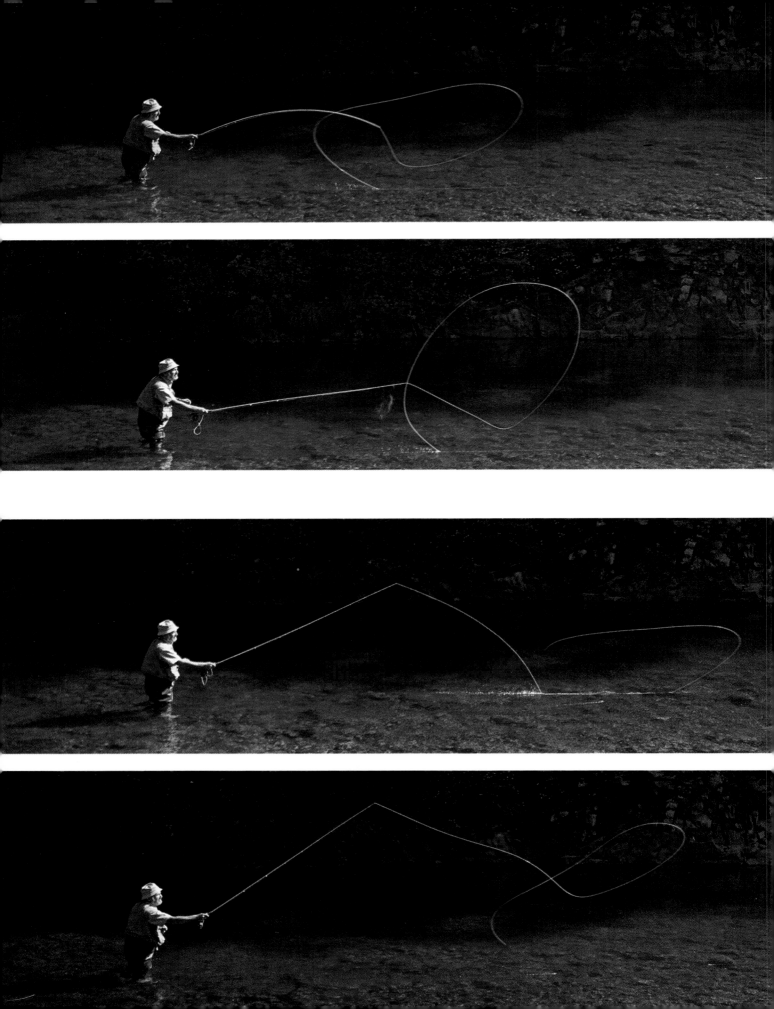

Good roll cast strokes drive the line forward with authority in an **elliptical loop**.

Poor roll cast strokes heave the line up in a **circular loop** *that flops to the water.*

Directing the power **low** *over the water produces a low-travelling loop, which is useful in a headwind.*

Directing the roll cast stroke **higher** *causes the elliptical loop to travel higher above the water, useful for a delicate presentation or in a following wind.*

help in forcing the rod to bend as well as in controlling the position of the rod. The roll cast motion can be likened to a chopping motion. Imagine a chopping block about waist high and at least 2 or 3 feet in front of you. Do this right now, without rod or line in your hand. Start with your hand about head high and stick a meat cleaver or a hatchet into the chopping block. Make a conscious effort to start this motion *with a decided pull*. Notice how abruptly your hand stops when it reaches the chopping block. A forced *stop* is an important part of the casting stroke. Now, with the same motion, stick only the tip end of the hatchet into the block. That little thrust (or point) directs the power in the cast toward the intended direction of the fly line. You've just made a beautiful roll casting stroke. This chopping-thrusting, pulling-pointing motion in the roll casting stroke is very similar to the power application in all flycasting strokes. Practice this pantomime exercise.

Notice the large circle-shaped loop in the accompanying photo and also the more elliptically shaped loop of the fly line in the comparison photo. Elliptical loops roll out the line much more efficiently than circular ones. Circular loops often roll the line *up* instead of driving it *out,* resulting in a collapsed line. These undesirable round loops usually form when you put an inadequate bend in the fly rod or apply power too early in the forward stroke. An early release of power is often the result of bringing the rod too far back (much beyond the one-o'clock position). Practice applying power both early and late in your casting stroke, noting the differences in the shapes of your casting loops. Also practice different casting stroke positions in order to vary the height of your cast. A cast directly over the water, as shown, is excellent for driving the line into the wind. A roll cast directed higher (tilt the casting arc back—raise the chopping block) benefits from a following wind, presents a fly more delicately and can be used to pick up a line from the water with minimum disturbance.

After you have practiced enough to be comfortable with the roll cast, try to start the forward cast just as the line falls behind the rod and while the line in the water is still

moving toward you. It is not hard to do. The moving fly line planes on top of the water, permitting longer and easier roll casts.

The Off-Shoulder Roll Cast

Notice that all of these roll casts must be made to the left of the line in the water. Casting to the right results in a tangled line. To direct the cast to the right side of the line in the water, you must cast from the left side of your body.

The simplest and most efficient technique for this off-shoulder casting is to tilt the rod to your left side *while maintaining your casting hand in the usual position on the right.* Simply rotate your casting hand so that the back of your hand is on top of the handle and your palm is facing out. Those of you who are using the Extended Finger Grip, simply rotate to the V Grip or the Palm Out Grip. This will cause the rod to tilt so that the rod tip and line are on the left side of your body. You may wish to tilt your forearm by moving your elbow out or even to lean your whole upper body if you need a more extreme angle. Now you can roll cast to the right of the line in the water. The key to this cast is keeping your casting hand in its usual position on the right side of your face. Do not work on the off-shoulder cast until you feel quite comfortable with the roll cast from the right side.

Spend at least a few hours with the roll cast, practicing various casting stroke positions and the off-shoulder cast. These few hours, along with some pantomime time, can be the foundation of an excellent basic casting stroke.

Left:

Start the **off-shoulder roll cast** *with your hand on the right side of your body and the rod tilted so that the rod tip and line are on your left.*

Right:

Aim the cast to the right of the line on the water to avoid tangling.

Left:

Keep an upright forearm and simply rotate your hand to the V Grip for a **moderate tilt** *to the left, the strongest off-shoulder position.*

Right:

Hold your elbow out from your body and slant your forearm and rod to the left for a **greater tilt** *toward your off shoulder.*

The Long Roll Cast

*Start the **long roll cast** by raising the rod to lift and plane the line toward you.*

Gently toss the line back to create a loop of line behind you. Toss as much line behind you as you can without fouling any obstacles.

The instant the line retouches the water, lean into a powerful roll cast stroke. Both rod and line are blurred by the rod thrust and a left hand haul.

Both hands have just completed their work as the elliptical loop drives out, ripping line from the water behind it. The loop takes off slightly upward for maximum distance.

As the line extends, it pulls the remaining slack through the guides for a 70-foot roll cast.

Experienced casters use a modification of the basic roll cast, to fish at suprisingly long distances—70 feet or more. Mastery of the long roll cast allows them to reach places others simply can't fish. Anglers using the long two-handed rods best known for Atlantic salmon fishing make this roll cast for even greater distances. I recommend that you develop the other basic casts described in this book before returning to this advanced roll casting technique.

The key to the long roll cast is to throw a larger loop of line behind the rod while still keeping a few feet of line and leader in the water in front of you. Generally, the larger the loop of line behind the rod (that obstructions permit), the farther you can cast. This larger loop is, in effect, a longer backcast.

Begin by sliding the line toward you as you would in the basic roll cast, then gently toss it back so that a few feet of fly line and the leader land in the water in front of you and a large loop of line falls behind the rod. Just as the line and leader retouch the water, drive the line forward using a powerful roll casting stroke. Tilt the casting arc back so that the cast has a high forward trajectory. The fly line should roll out in an elliptical loop. With practice, you will develop the feel of tossing the line back with just the right amount of power and perfect the timing of the forward cast.

After you have learned the double haul (discussed in Chapter 8, "The Double Haul"), you can use a left hand pull to add even more distance to this cast. Double taper lines are best suited to the long roll cast, but you can do very well with a weight forward line by shooting line for extra distance. □

5

The Basic Flycast

The most difficult part of flycasting to communicate and to learn is the feel of correctly applying power to the rod and line. Lee Wulff, when asked to describe that feel, replied, "Can you describe for me the taste of an apple?" He then explained, as I must, that the only way to really learn flycasting is to experience it. Before you run to the nearest pond or lawn, however, allow me to offer some goals, some descriptions, some analogies and one very important exercise that will hasten your discovery of the wonderful feel of casting a fly.

Loading the rod correctly is the first and perhaps the most important step in developing the feel of flycasting. Even many experienced flyfishers have somehow bypassed this basic discipline. The word "loading" is an incomplete description of the actual motion. A better description might well be loading *and unloading* the rod. Forcing the rod to first load (bend) and then unload (rapidly straighten) is the entire motion. *It's probably a different motion than most of you think.* The crucial part of this movement is a rather abrupt stop of your casting hand that forces the rod to unload. Casting instructors use all kinds of phrases to describe this loading and unloading of the rod. "Stopping the rod," "flipping the tip," "power snap," "wrist snap," "hand snap," "popping the tip," and my own favorite, *"whumping the rod,"* are just some of the attempts to communicate this relatively simple bending-unbending movement of a flexible fly rod. One exercise, however, communicates rod unloading better than all of these words.

Assemble a rod without a line. Do it now, right in your home. Hold the rod in front of you horizontally, with the palm of your hand facing up. Now, using a very short stroke, force the rod to bend—then stop your hand abruptly. You will feel a decided *"whump"* as the rod unloads. Notice that you can load and unload the rod with just a few inches of hand movement. Hold the rod firmly. Notice how much easier it is to load the rod with a stiff wrist. Now make a longer, heavier stroke and stop it hard. Do it backward and forward. Now softer. Softer. Now make an extremely gentle whump—almost imperceptible. That's all there is to it. The whump feels much smoother and less pronounced when you are actually casting with a fly line.

Never again cast a fly or even wave a fly rod back and forth without this forced stop. Reread this very important rod loading introduction. Practice this funny hand stop, this correct casting stroke, with and without a rod. Spend some pantomime time.

*Hold the rod horizontally in front of you and force it to load and unload with a **whump**. Without a line, the rod bends more from the stop than from the forward stroke.*

The pick up and lay down cast, as its name implies, consists of one backcast and one forward cast, culminating with the line extended in front. It is commonly used in fishing and is fundamental in flycasting.

Find a nice lawn and, after a short review of the whumping exercise on both backcasts and forward casts, string the rod and stretch out about 25 feet of floating fly line in front of you. Use a squared stance and hold the fly line against the rod handle with the middle finger or the forefinger of your casting hand. Your arm should be comfortably at your side with your forearm and rod pointing to the practice fly on the ground. Keeping a very firm wrist, cast the line up and back, stopping the rod at about the one-o'clock position so that the line loops off the rod tip. Hesitate so that the line looping to the rear has time to almost straighten out.

*The **pick up and lay down cast** starts with the rod tip pointed low and the line extended straight in front.*

Raising the rod planes the line on the water at the start of the pick up.

The rod has just been stopped at one o'clock, and the loop forms as the line races over the rod tip. Planing the line has freed it from the glassy surface without any disturbance.

A momentary pause allows the backcast to straighten. This is the instant when the forward cast begins.

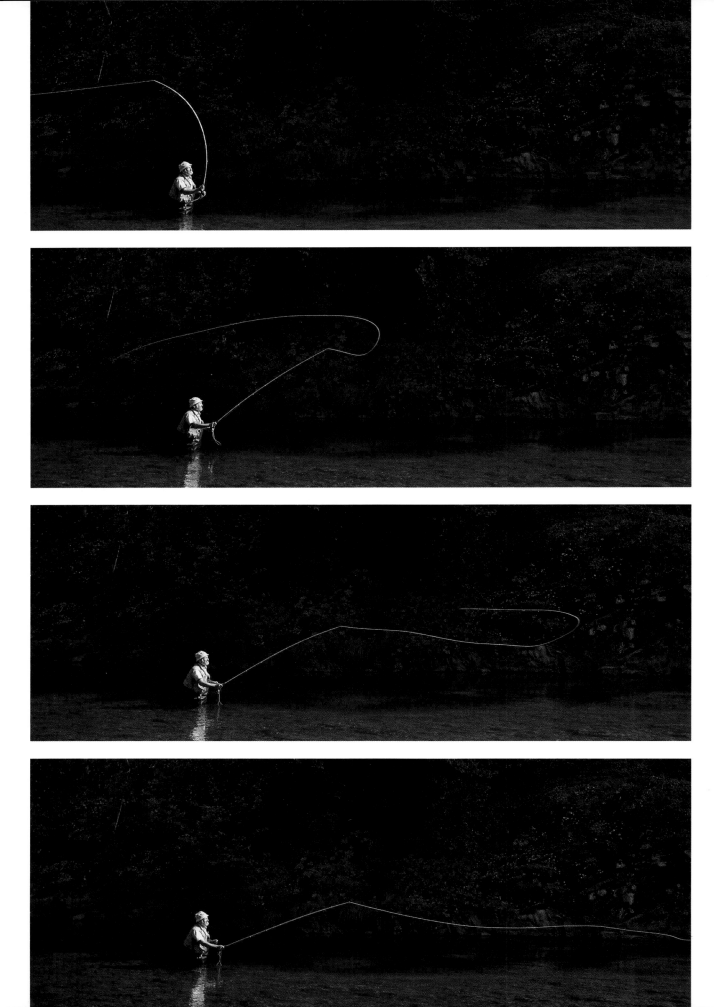

The hand pulls the rod into the forward stroke.

Anchored by the stopped rod tip, the line rolls forward to form the loop.

Both legs of this good loop are parallel as it extends. The rod has begun lowering for the lay down.

To complete the lay down, the rod continues to follow the line as it falls gently to the water.

Now cast the rod down and forward to about the eleven- or ten-o'clock position to roll the line off the rod tip in front of you. After the loop has formed and is well out in front of the rod, follow the line with the tip of the rod as it falls to the ground.

When casting on water, begin the backcast by slowly sliding the line in the water a foot or two toward you. This movement frees the line from the surface tension of the water, making your backcast easier to get airborne. Planing the line in this manner before you pick it up also minimizes water disturbance, an important consideration when you are fishing.

Remember to load the rod as you *sling* the line back and then forward. Although you must grip the handle firmly to load the rod, do not squeeze too hard. Try to hold the rod gently so that you can feel the subtle whump on this short cast and to avoid tiring your hand. Yes, it is possible to keep a firm grip and a firm wrist and still hold the rod gently.

Do not think of throwing the line with your hand. Think "I must use the tip of the rod to cast the line." A.J. McClane, the renowned angler and author, uses this excellent description: "You should have the feeling that you are throwing the rod tip into the cast." If the loop in the forward cast is too fat (deep) or fails to form at all, stop the rod higher (to narrow the casting arc) or put a little stronger load in the rod. If the loop in the forward cast is too narrow or hits itself or the rod (a tailing loop), stop the rod a bit lower (to widen the casting arc), or make a gentler whump. After you develop the feel of a good loop rolling off the rod tip in the forward cast, strive for exactly that same feel in the backcast.

From time to time, drop your right foot back so that you can watch your backcast (and, now and then, your wrist). The line should be almost straight behind you before you start the forward cast. Watching the backcast can help your timing, as well as enable you to monitor the direction and loop shape of the fly line.

*Made with the rod in a horizontal plane, the **sidearm cast** directs the line under obstacles on the far bank.*

The sidearm stroke forms a horizontal loop that keeps line and fly low to the water.

Extending low over the surface, the line carries the fly to its target under the obstructions. A very low line will even skip the fly under especially low cover.

Tilt the rod slightly to the right (away from you) as you cast. This angles the casting loop so the line on the top of the loop is less likely to hit the bottom of the loop or the rod. You can also use a different maneuver to prevent the line from hitting itself or the rod. Tilt the rod slightly to the right only during the backcast and return the rod to vertical for the forward cast. The backcast travels slightly to the right of the forward cast, and the momentary pause as you return the rod to vertical can actually help your timing.

Vary the amount of power you apply to the rod; notice how little force you need to cast this short line. Try to load and unload the rod smoothly. Work on varying the position and the size of the casting arc. Try some sidearm casts. The sidearm cast is useful in fishing because the line traveling low to the water encounters less wind velocity and zips under overhanging trees or bushes.

Experimenting and change are essential to good practice in flycasting. Don't allow yourself to get into a groove—making the same cast over and over. After practicing a casting stroke for a while, do something different. By all means, do it wrong. It's almost impossible to flycast well without knowing how to cast badly. Learn how to cast tailing loops and how to cast a line without loops (non-loops). Vary your timing on backcasts and forward casts. Go too fast. Go too slow. Change makes practice sessions more interesting and hastens the learning process. Change is one of life's lessons that also applies to fishing. Many fishers succumb to the inertia of sameness. They continue to use the same fishing methods over and over again even when they're not successful. The reward for changing is not just more fish, it is also a richer fishing experience.

*In the **false cast**, the forward loop must be high enough to avoid touching the water as it extends.*

The slightly bent rod shows that the backcast was begun slightly before the line reached the straight position shown here.

The False Cast

In a false cast, the forward cast is not allowed to fall to the water. Just as the loop straightens out in front, the fly line is cast back again. We use the false cast to change distance and direction, and frequently to dry out a floating fly. Mastering the timing of this back-and-forth movement of the line takes a little practice. Everyone develops the correct timing with just a few hours of practice. It may help to think in terms of developing a rhythm in fly casting. Make a mental note of the time it takes for the forward cast to roll out and allow an equal amount of time for the backcast. The longer the cast, the more time it takes to straighten, and therefore, the slower the rhythm. Bending your knees and swaying with your whole body as you cast might help you develop the rhythm. Every now and then, drop your right foot back and watch several consecutive false casts. A good general rule in fishing is to use as few false casts as possible. In this exercise, however, make as many as five or six false casts before presenting the fly. Practice with varying lengths of fly line.

Though it continues to fall slightly as you back-cast, the line does not touch the water on a proper false cast.

As the **off-shoulder cast** begins, the rod hand is in its normal position on your right side while the rod is canted so that the rod tip and line are on your left side.

The rod hand remains on your right side as the backcast is made over your left side.

The line flies safely past on your left side—ideal in a wind coming from your right.

The Off-Shoulder Cast

The off-shoulder cast—analogous to the off-shoulder roll cast you learned in Chapter 4, "The Roll Cast"—is needed in many fishing and casting situations. Crosswinds that blow the line and fly toward you (i.e., from your right if you're right handed), obstructions such as rocks and trees, and the safety of your partner when fishing from a boat, are just a few of the many reasons to perfect this important cast. The across-the-body cast, the back hand cast from a sideways stance, casting with the left hand and even turning around to present a backcast to the fish are all methods for casting on the left side. The off-shoulder cast, however, is the most effective.

This technique simply requires tilting the rod to the left side while maintaining your rod hand in its usual position on the right side of your face. You can do this most easily by simply rotating your rod and hand to the V Grip or the Palm Out Grip. Keep your hand well in front of you and high enough (about eye high) so that the rod will pass over your head. Try to keep your forearm relatively vertical for most comfortable casting. You may, however, tilt your forearm as well as the rod by moving your elbow out, or even lean your whole upper body if you need an extreme angle. Make sure that your right hand stays in its usual strong position on the right side of your face through-out the cast. This cast is somewhat simpler to conceive than to do. Most people feel comfortable with it after a couple of hours of practice or a day's fishing with a right hand wind.

*Use the **off-shoulder cast** from a boat to keep the line safely away from your partner.*

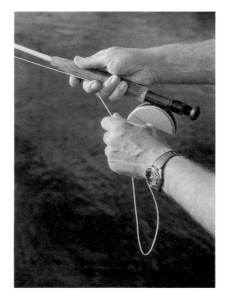

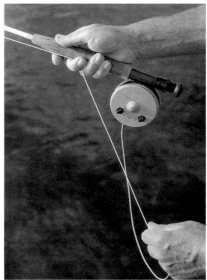

The Line Hand

This is a good time to begin training your left (line) hand. Until now you've anchored the fly line with your casting hand against the handle of the fly rod. Now, hold it tightly in your left hand. Do *not* hold the line with both hands; your left hand serves as the sole anchor point for the back end of the line. *Hold the line tightly during the entire casting stroke.* It also acts as the control hand while extending line in false casting. Extend line on the forward cast by letting line slip through your left hand only after the rod unloads and the loop is out in front of the rod. Later, you may wish to practice extending line on the backcast as well.

Try pulling the line with your left hand, separating your hands as you lift line off the water for a backcast. This motion, called the single haul, helps straighten the line and adds speed to the backcast. Remember to start slowly, planing the floating line on top of the water before you pick it up to make your backcast. Also use a longer casting stroke by starting with your rod tip low, pointing at the fly in the water.

To retrieve the fly line, hook the line with the middle finger or forefinger of your casting hand against the rod handle and strip the line in with your left hand. Always strip the line from *in back of your casting hand.* Reaching in front of your casting hand will cause you to lose control of the fly line. This stripping technique to retrieve and control the fly line is an integral part of flyfishing. One of the beauties of flyfishing is the extreme simplicity of the line handling. We do not have to work through complicated gear systems and other mechanical marvels. Ours is a direct connection between line and fly and fish.

Another small but important job of the left hand is to guide the line evenly and with tension onto the reel as the right hand turns the reel handle (the right hand guides the line, of course, if you choose to reel with your left hand). This may be a little awkward at first, but will quickly become almost automatic.

*In the **single haul**, the left hand starts to pull as the right hand loads the rod for the backcast.*

As the right hand completes the backcast, the left hand pull has helped boost the line into the air.

Left:
Hook the line *with the middle finger or forefinger of your rod hand to gain control of the line before retrieving.*

Right:
Retrieve by pulling the line from behind your rod hand.

To **shoot line**, hold the line firmly during the power stroke.

Release the line when the loop has formed in front of the rod.

Shooting Line

After you can comfortably false cast 35 to 40 feet of fly line, try shooting line for distance. Strip an extra 8 to 10 feet of line from the reel onto the grass in front of you. Hold the line tightly in your left hand. False cast until you have good control of the line in the air. On the final forward cast—the presentation cast—let go of the line with your left hand, and the extra line at your feet will shoot out of the rod. Do *not* let go of the line until the loop has formed in front of the rod.

When shooting line, use a wider casting arc to compensate for the additional rod bend in this longer cast. Make sure you whump the rod and that you are still casting good loops—especially on the final, or presentation cast. End with your rod tip high. Direct the unloading of the rod *in the intended direction of the fly line.* This is excellent advice for all flycasting strokes. Try to shoot even more line. Try to false cast with more line. See how far you can cast. Have some fun experimenting.

Bring yourself back to earth by making some shorter, more controlled casts before you conclude this practice session. This is a good time to look over the chapters on good form and mechanics. ☐

A good loop pulls all the slack out through the guides.

6

The Application
of Power

The basic feel of casting that beginning
flycasters must learn is that of loading and
unloading the rod—the feel of stopping the rod
in order to propel the line and fly. You have
learned the basic feel of looping out the line in
the preceding chapter. You must now develop a
more subtle feel—refining this loading motion to
control the loop shape and to accommodate dif-
fering rod loads. This chapter offers various
descriptions, analogies and exercises to help you
learn the proper application of power.

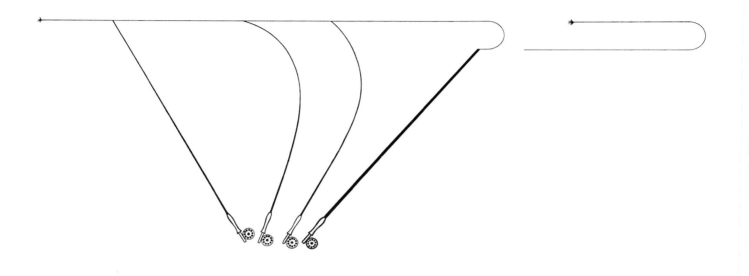

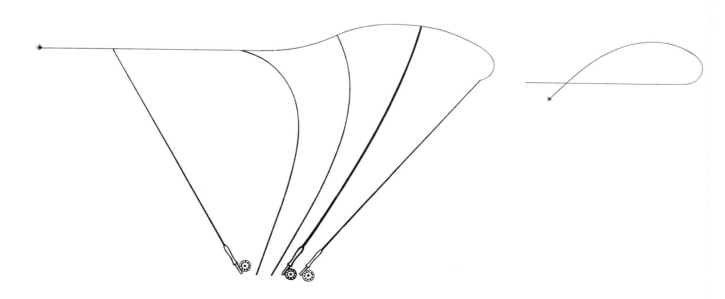

Intermediate and advanced casters commonly experience the problem of a tailing loop, which is usually caused by an improper application of power (see Chapter 1, "The Mechanics of Flycasting"). This poor loop shape almost invariably results from the rod unloading too early in the casting stroke. The correct power application is a constant *acceleration* throughout the casting stroke to maintain the straight-line path of the rod tip. If you have trouble with a tailing loop, consider the following suggestions: 1) Think of unloading the rod with the rod tip stopped *below* the path of the fly line. 2) Maintain the casting stroke until the tip of the rod is past your hand and *below* the path of the fly line. 3) Try not to unload the rod until all of the fly line in the air is moving in the correct direction. 4) Think of the casting stroke as fluid and continuous rather than as a jarring or jolting motion. The abrupt stop (unloading the rod) that I mentioned earlier is simply the conclusion of a continuous application of power.

All of that sounds more formidable than it really is. A little practice slinging the fly line back and forth with a *smoother* whump and perhaps a longer *whu-u-mp* will probably solve the problem for most of you.

One of my favorite descriptions of the power application in flycasting was written in about 1930 by Paul Young, the noted Michigan rod-maker. He described it something like this: "Imagine an apple stuck on the sharpened end of a long, very flexible switch or rod. In order to throw this heavy apple, start very slowly, completely bending (loading) the rod, then accelerate, and finally—stop (unload), slinging the apple toward its target. An erratic power application or power that is applied too soon would result in the apple slipping prematurely from the rod and falling to the ground." Another analogy, for those of you who have fished with bait, is the way you apply power when casting soft baits that do not hold well on the hook. You need a smooth start and constant acceleration during the cast to prevent the bait from slipping off. Golfers may relate somewhat to "hitting from the top," that is, applying power too early in the swing rather than achieving the maximum clubhead speed at the point of

A longer whu-u-mp allows the rod to unload below the straight-line path of the fly line.

*Unloading the rod too early in the stroke results in a **tailing loop** or the line colliding with the rod.*

impact. You might try thinking of a fly rod as a very flexible golf club.

Imagine the loading and unloading of the rod as smooth, even and continuous. At this point (after you have learned to properly whump the rod), never think of punching, popping, poking or hitting the rod or line. Instead, think of *slinging* the line. Sam Snead, when asked what he was thinking as he made his golf swing, answered, "Oily." I suspect Sam would do very well with a fly rod.

Think of keeping the rod bent throughout the stroke, of continuously pulling the line. Imagine first loading the rod, then—and only then—slinging the line off the tip of the rod in a rolling loop, or pulling the rod until *all* of the fly line in the air is pulled straight and moving, and only then unloading the rod. Most flycasters have more trouble with long casts than short ones, with softer rods than with stiff ones, with a hard casting stroke than a gentle one. Try to keep the bend in the rod *longer*. Think of casting *heavier* rather than quicker when you need more power. The longer casting stroke needed for the bigger bend in the rod simply requires a longer whump. Something like a *whu-u-u-mp!*

Practice this smooth unloading of the rod. Be sure, also, to teach yourself to cast a pronounced tailing loop by whumping the rod too quickly or too soon. I promise that, with practice, you will soon know the sweet feel of a really good flycast.

Variable Flycasting Strokes

Most flycasters, including many with considerable experience, limit their casting and fishing by using a single type of flycasting stroke. Their early instruction probably started with "eleven o'clock to two o'clock" or "always attempt to stop the rod at twelve o'clock in order to get a high backcast" or one of the many other cliches common in flycasting instruction. They usually spend a lot of time trying to find a rod with the correct action or the right combination of line weight and rod stiffness to fit their particular casting stroke.

Maintain the casting stroke until the rod tip is below the path of the line.

Unloading the rod too soon or too quickly causes the rod tip to stop above the path of the fly line. The result will be a tailing loop.

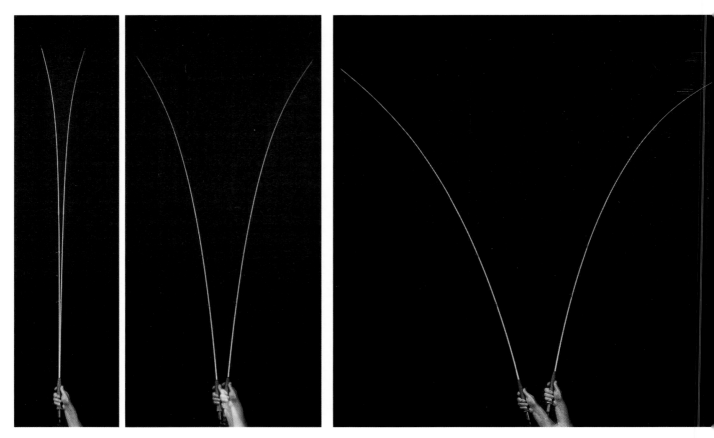

On the other hand, all really good casters, consciously or unconsciously, go beyond this limited, mechanical approach to develop the feel of casting a good loop with varying rod positions, rod loads and rod actions. In short, they are able to adjust their casting stroke to handle the variety of casting situations that fishing invariably presents. For example, casting the considerable weight of 80 feet of fly line obviously requires a different casting stroke than casting only 5 or 10 feet of fly line.

Varying your casting stroke is not as difficult as you might think. In fact, as you explore the full range of casting strokes, the feel of looping a fly line back and forth with a long, flexible fly rod will really start making sense, and flycasting will actually become easier. In previous chapters I referred to narrow and wide casting arcs. Let's take a closer look at them. I promise you that, at this stage of your flycasting education, you're going to have some fun.

Start with an adaptation of the rod whumping exercise described in the previous chapter. Assemble a rod without a line. Hold the rod horizontally in front of you and, using a very short stroke, whump the tip—only the very tip—of the rod. Remember to lock your wrist and use a very abrupt stop to unload the rod. Notice that you need to move your hand only a few inches to make this stroke. Do it gently. Too much power will bend the rod too far down. Only the top 2 feet or so of the rod should bend appreciably. This tip casting stroke (without a fly line) is a kind of flicking, flipping, bouncing motion of the rod tip—a gentle, quick whump. Now, using a somewhat wider casting arc, force the rod to load and unload down into the middle of the rod. Use a harder whump—a bit longer *whu-u-mp*. Finally, use an even wider casting stroke and more force, loading the rod into the butt—right down to the handle. The whole rod, butt through tip, should be bending. This butt cast is an even longer *whu-u-u-mp*.

Holding the rod horizontally allows you to see as well as feel the loading and unloading of a fly rod from a tip cast through to the butt cast—the entire range of casting strokes. Do it right now in your own home.

On the Lawn

After you briefly review the variable stroke rod loading exercise, string the rod with a floating fly line (with leader and yarn fly). Work out no more than 10 to 15 feet of fly line and try the tip cast. Imagine that you are allowing only the very tip of the fly rod to bend and that the rest of the rod must remain straight. Keep your wrist firm to maintain a very narrow casting stroke (casting arc) and to force the rod to bend only at the tip. Start with a pick up and lay down cast, concentrating only on the forward cast. Try to feel just the tip of the rod bending and slinging the line in a very narrow loop. Notice that the feel of whumping the tip of the rod is much more subtle with the weight of a fly line. Hold the rod gently so that you can feel the rod working. Remember that you can hold the rod gently while still keeping a firm wrist. You must also cast gently. Too much power bends the rod too far down. Cast this narrow loop high in the air, off the very top of the rod, aiming your cast a foot or two above the water or lawn. Continue to practice this pick up and lay down cast until you can easily and consistently cast a narrow loop. Now concentrate on the backcast and attempt to develop the same feel as in the forward cast. Be sure to tilt the rod slightly to the right during the backcast so that the line does not hit the rod. Practice false casting. Try doing it horizontally for a few casts (in front of you, as you did in the exercise without a line). You can easily see both the backcast and forward cast without twisting your neck. Use various amounts of power. Notice how little power is required to cast this short line and that too much power results in a poor loop. Extend some line. You may be surprised how far you can cast with this gentle, slinging tip cast.

*Gentle **tip casts** for short distances flex the rod primarily at the tip. Rod motion blurs the tip in this photo.*

Because they start high in the air off the tip of the rod, tip cast loops may have to be directed slightly downward at the target.

At about 25 to 30 feet, casting with just the tip of the rod becomes increasingly difficult. At about this point, the weight of the line or the amount of power you apply causes the rod to bend farther down toward the middle of the rod. You have to increase the size of the casting arc to avoid tailing loops. Make a distinct effort to whu-u-mp the rod a bit harder and nearer the middle of the fly rod, as you increase the size of your casting stroke. Notice that the line now feel like it is flowing off the middle of the rod instead of the tip, that the loop is not as high as with the tip cast, and that the stronger, longer whu-u-mp in the stiffer middle of the rod generates more line speed. Spend some time with the tip cast and the middle-of-the-rod cast using various lengths of fly line and different amounts of power.

The butt cast is the other extreme in fly-casting strokes. This sweeping, full-stroke cast requires a forceful loading of the heavy butt section of the fly rod. The casting motion of the pick up and lay down butt cast is almost identical to the pulling-pointing roll casting stroke. Review the chopping block analogy we used for the roll cast in Chapter 4. Be sure to pull your hand through the casting stroke as far as possible before pointing. Generally, the pulling motion loads the fly rod, and the pointing stop of the rod tip completes the unloading. Never push the rod. Imagine that you are pulling a 2-foot length of rope through the air and smacking it down on the chopping block well out in front of you. All fly casting strokes should start with a decided *pulling* motion—the hand before the rod. Pantomime this movement with imaginary hatchets and ropes before you begin casting.

Middle-of-the-rod casts for *medium distances cause the rod to bend farther down. The casting motion blurs the top half of the rod.*

Middle-of-the-rod casts form loops that start lower in the air than tip cast loops.

For the next practice, work with a shooting taper or at least 30 to 35 feet of floating fly line because the rod should be fully loaded. Once again, start with the pick up and lay down cast. Direct the loop as close to the water or lawn as possible. After a fairly high backcast, start the forward cast with your hand held high (about even with the top of your head). Pull the rod down and over, sweeping the rod down as far as possible and pointing to the place where you expect the fly to land. Maintain a firm wrist, forcing the rod to bend well into the butt. Imagine that you are putting a casting loop into the rod itself. Direct this *loop in the rod* (this unloading of the rod) toward the intended direction of the fly line. Try to get the loop as low as possible, with the line rolling out right along the water or lawn. This cast is simpler than it sounds. Review the text, take a good look at the pictures and, after a few minutes of pantomiming the stroke, cast a fly. It's an easy cast that most of you will learn in a very short time.

This pick up and lay down butt cast is a superb cast for presenting the fly under extremely windy conditions. The stiff butt section of the rod provides tremendous line speed, and the loop rolling very low on the water offers maximum control when the wind is

*Powerful **butt casts** flex the rod all the way down. Almost the entire rod is blurred.*

Butt cast loops, formed by a bend far down in the rod, generally start low in the air.

*Start all casting strokes with a decided **pulling motion**.*

75

*For the **Madison cast**, pull the rod down, forcing a bend well into the butt. Make a pulling-pointing motion.*

Traveling fast and low over the water, the Madison cast loop is frequently pointed.

blowing. Sometimes it's called the Madison cast because the Madison River in Montana frequently has very strong winds, and many of the fishing guides teach their clients this presentation cast before they float and fish the river.

After you develop the feel of this pick up and lay down butt cast, aim your forward cast higher in the air. Please notice that you need a large casting arc for this butt cast and that you must tilt the entire casting stroke backward to make the higher forward cast. Strive for the same feeling of casting off the butt of the rod that you experienced in the pick up and lay down butt cast. The casting loop travels lower in the air (closer to your casting hand) than with the tip cast or the middle-of-the-rod cast because of the additional bend in the rod. The casting loop is frequently pointed, like a tipped over V, while loops from the tip cast and the middle-of-the-rod cast are usually rounded, like a tipped over U. Although the pointed loops generally have more speed, both loop shapes are excellent. You will need a little practice to change the position of the casting stroke for the higher forward cast. If you have difficulty, revert to the pick up and lay down cast to get the proper feel again. This powerful butt cast is very useful whenever you want great line speed, as in distance casting or casting in very windy conditions. You also need this wide arc casting stroke whenever you put a big bend in a rod (e.g., an overloaded rod or one that is designed with a very slow or butt action). Once again, the keys to the butt cast are a wide casting stroke, forcing the rod to bend at the butt and a long, sweeping, pointing *whu-u-u-mp*.

Try these casts on different fly rods. After a few hours with these exercises you may change your perspective on rod action, and you will certainly have made substantial progress in developing the special feel that is flycasting.   □

7

The Fly Rod

As the medium through which we feel and control the line, fly and fish, the fly rod has received a great deal of loving attention over the years. This simple, flexible rod is the very essence of flyfishing.

Unfortunately, the writings of generations of anglers and craftsmen and the advertising hype of some rod companies have turned this wonderfully simple tool into a nightmare of complexity. Rod action—the manner in which a rod bends—has somehow come to be a mysterious and indefinable concept. Various new rod materials have only added to the confusion. A recent flyfishing book finished a chapter on rods with this amazing statement: "For the student who wishes to analyze the subject scientifically, the physics of movement which apply to dynamic rod action and kinetic line travel are contained in Newton's Law of Motion and Einstein's Theory of Relativity." Clearly, the case has been overstated!

I'll define the workings of a fly rod in simpler terms and explain how rod action and rod stiffness affect fishing and casting. I'll use the words BUTT and TIP to describe the parts of a fly rod, and the words STIFF and SOFT to describe a fly rod's resistance to bending.

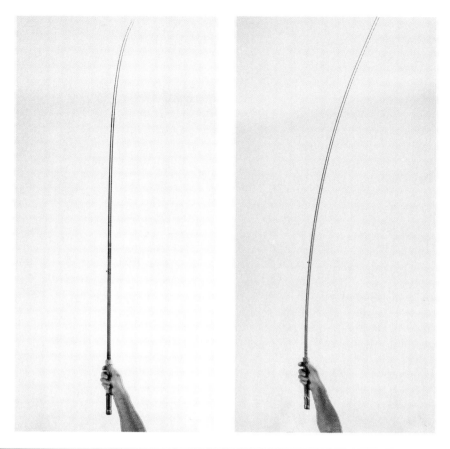

Rod *action* can be defined in terms of *where* the bending takes place. A TIP ACTION rod bends mostly at the tip; a BUTT ACTION rod, at the butt of the rod. One highly desirable compromise, or combination, of these two basic actions is called PROGRESSIVE ACTION. A progressive action rod bends primarily near the tip with light loads and bends progressively farther down the rod to butt action as the load increases. The load is a result of the weight of the line outside the tiptop and the amount of power applied by the caster, both of which make the rod bend.

Rod *stiffness*—resistance to bending—ranges from stiff to soft. Usually a reference to rod stiffness is within the context of a given line weight. Thus a fly rod that balances best with a 6-weight fly line could be described as either stiff or soft. A rod that is overly stiff with a 6-weight line will more properly balance with a 7-weight line. The basic overall stiffness of a fly rod, of course, determines its appropriate line weight (see the rod table in Chapter 2, "Equipment").

For hooking and playing fish, the advantage of one rod action or rod stiffness over another (within a given line weight) is minimal. Rod action and rod stiffness are most important in their relationships to flycasting.

Rod Stiffness in Flycasting

The stiffness of a fly rod determines the range at which it casts most effectively. A stiffer rod generally casts a longer line because it produces greater line speed. This additional speed also helps on windy days and often has advantages in fly presentation. On the other hand, shorter casts can be made more comfortably with a rod soft enough to bend easily with the lesser weight of a shorter line. Most of us are creatures of habit, with strong tendencies to put ourselves into the same fishing situations all the time. For example, some trout fishers like to get as close to their quarry as possible, often making casts of only 10 to 15 feet. Others stay back and make 60-foot presentations. Some fishing situations also demand long or short casts; for example, large rivers and lakes generally demand longer casts than small

Left:
Tip action *rods, like the bamboo one shown here, flex primarily near the tip while the stiff butt remains straight.*

Right:
Butt action *rods bend much farther down even under a light load. The tip remains quite straight.*

*A **progressive action** rod under medium load flexes smoothly with butt intact for an easy pick up.*

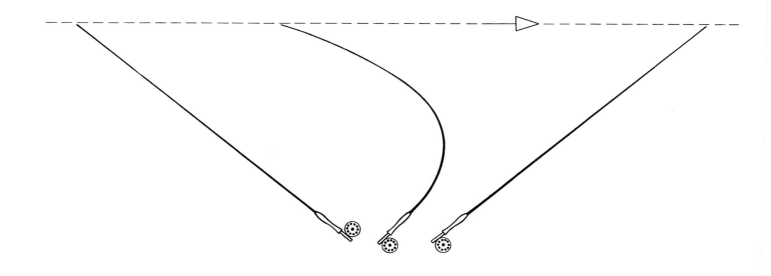

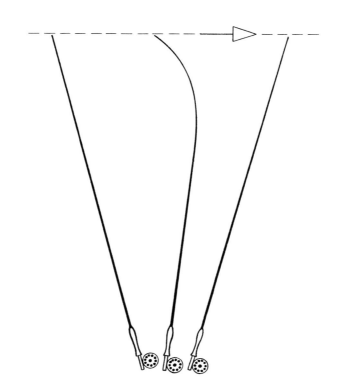

*A soft **butt action** rod is best with a wide casting stroke.*

*A **tip action** rod works best with a narrow casting stroke.*

streams. Try to evaluate your own needs and inclinations. Now factor in another personal preference—the slow, easy, full casting stroke of a soft rod versus the more forceful loading, narrower stroke of a stiffer rod—and you should be close to making a decision on the sort of fly rod stiffness that's right for you.

Experienced anglers often underweight or overweight a particular rod by changing the line to make the rod feel stiffer or softer. A fly rod rated for a 6-weight line is effectively stiffer with a lighter 5-weight line, and feels relatively softer with a heavier 7-weight line. You should also be aware that rod manufacturers often differ among themselves in rating rods for line sizes. Be sure to try any new rod with more than one line size.

Rod Action in Flycasting

Now let's consider rod *action*—where a rod bends—in relation to a flycasting stroke. The butt cast, with its wide arc casting stroke, requires a full bend in the fly rod to maintain the straight-line path of the rod tip that's needed for good casting. You can generally make that full bend more easily in a fly rod inclined toward butt action. Flyfishers who limit themselves to the full stroke butt cast will almost invariably choose a rod that bends easily in the butt—a butt action rod. On the other hand, those who like to fire the line off the tip of the rod, using a narrow casting stroke, would do best with a tip action rod.

Most of the better fly rods available today are designed with some version of progressive action, with varying degrees of emphasis on tip and butt. Although progressive action appears to be a poor compromise between tip action and butt action rods, the opposite is usually true. A good progressive action fly rod enhances the tip and butt casting strokes and, of course, is ideal for the angler who uses a wide variety of casting strokes.

Personally, I evaluate a fly rod's action by the way the rod handles the full range of flycasting strokes. A tip action rod in which the butt is too stiff and a butt action rod in which the butt is too soft both have limiting actions. My choice is a progressive action rod that is

*Under a light load, the **progressive action** rod flexes near the tip.*

Under a medium load, the rod flexes farther down toward the middle.

Under a heavy load, the rod takes a deep bend into its butt section.

nicely balanced between tip and butt. The rod should be sensitive enough to let me feel the tip working while I'm casting a short line with a tip casting stroke. As I lengthen line and increase power, the rod must comfortably cast off its middle without the tip giving up or the butt beginning to hinge. During both of these casts, the butt section should be stiff enough to stay intact, with no feeling of any appreciable bend. As I apply more power still, I want to feel the rod bend well down into the butt section. In this butt cast, I'd like the bend to progress through the rod—from butt to tip— with no feeling of inconsistency or hinging. I can imagine putting into the fly rod itself a casting loop that sweeps through the rod and out into the line. Such a beautifully balanced rod casts smoothly and well from a tip cast to a butt cast, from leader-only range to the full length of a fly line.

Is there a perfect fly rod? Of course not. Fortunately, most of us have a wonderful time searching for the ultimate fly rod. Over the years, fly rod action has been relatively unchanged. Some old bamboo rods have excellent progressive action and, to this day, cast and fish well. Although bamboo and fiberglass fly rods are still made and are fine fishing tools, I believe the new graphite rods are a substantial step forward. Modern fly rods, like medicine and tennis rackets and some of the other fruits of man's progress, are superb. Super-light graphite rods handle the full range of fishing situations exceedingly well and have tremendous casting range, comfortably loading and casting from short through long distances. I might add that a large percentage of fly rods available today have excellent design and the type of progressive action that approaches my description of the perfect fly rod.

As you spend some time with the various casting strokes, you will develop your own perspective on rod action. The variable stroke whumping exercise doubles as an excellent way to determine rod action—a great fly shop "wiggle." ☐

8

The Double Haul

The double haul is an integral part of flycasting, and every serious flyfisher should master this important and easily learned technique. A.J. McClane called it "the greatest contribution to casting technique in the last century." This maneuver consists of pulling the line with the left hand (the line hand) during both the backcast and the forward cast to increase the speed of the fly line in the air. Developed by tournament casters for distance events, it is now used by flyfishers all over the world in almost every fishing situation.

Most flyfishers still think of the double haul as solely a method for increasing their distance, and may not recognize that it produces additional and probably even more important advantages. The increased line speed created by the double haul improves line control at all distances—control that aids in presenting the fly, overcoming wind conditions, threading a backcast through or over obstacles, unrolling long leaders and much more. Besides increasing distance and line control, the double haul makes casting easier. The line hand pull helps to straighten and position the fly line, and it reduces the work of the rod hand. The double haul offers most casters another very important advantage: added control of the fly line between the line hand and the first guide of the fly rod. A line hand trained in the double haul automatically maintains the taut line required for good flycasting. In short, the double haul makes almost every aspect of flycasting easier and more efficient.

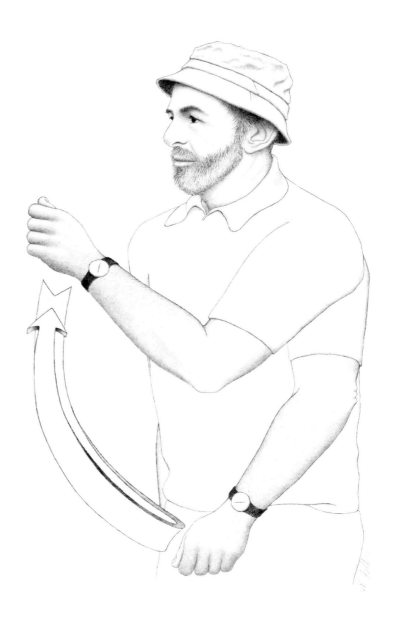

Learning the double haul appears to be such a difficult and time-consuming discipline that many flyfishers hesitate to attempt it. Earlier I stated that the double haul is easy to learn. It is. The average flycaster can master this exciting casting technique in a very short time by using a shooting taper and some pantomime exercises to teach muscle memory.

Before describing the exercises, I want to say a few words about shooting tapers. The shooting taper and running line combination, an extreme version of the weight forward line, is designed for maximum distance. Shooting tapers are presently sold in 30-foot lengths and are most often used with running lines of either monofilament or special small-diameter fly line. The 30-foot shooting taper provides the weight for casting, and the small-diameter running line allows a long shoot of 60 feet or more. Because shooting tapers, which come in various densities for different sink rates, are short and have built-in attaching loops, they are very easy to exchange. Thus, one reel set up with running line can be used for the full spectrum of floating and sinking lines. The effectiveness of this versatile distance line, now used all over the world in a wide variety of fishing situations, can no longer be questioned by serious flyfishers. It is also a superb piece of equipment for developing a good casting stroke and especially for learning the double haul.

The double haul is a little like rubbing your stomach while patting your head. At first it seems impossible, but after a few minutes, something goes "click" and it becomes easy. Pantomime exercises provide an easy way to learn how both hands work together in this casting technique. Most of you will learn the hand movements in less than 15 minutes. Stand up right now and do them. The only genuine obstacle to learning the double haul is a reluctance to try.

You must first learn a new word, as the motion it describes is the key to this exercise. The magic word is *downup*. It is not down-up. *Downup* is one word and one movement of the line (left) hand. Try it using only your left hand. Start with your left hand in front of your chest. Pull your hand *downup*—to your left hip and back up to your chest.

*This bouncing **downup** motion of the left hand is the key to learning the double haul.*

1.

In the **double haul pantomime**, this is the starting position for the backcast. Think through the next movement.

2.

Your right hand casts back at the same time your left hand goes downup.

4.

Now, **pantomime the forward cast**. Think through the next movement.

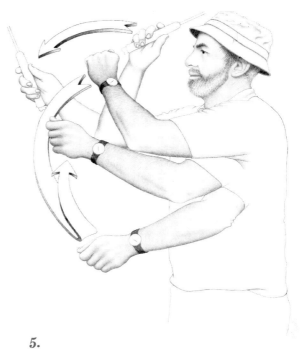

5.

Your right hand casts forward at the same time your left goes downup.

3.

Conclude the backcast with both hands together, your left slightly below your right.

Imagine that your hand strikes a needle near your hip and rebounds immediately. I can't stress this strongly enough: your hand must literally bounce at the bottom of the *downup* stroke. Practice this movement for a minute or two, using only your left hand, before going on to the next step.

Now drop your right foot back so that you can sway a bit as you cast. A long casting stroke is also easier to make with this stance. Imagine that you are holding the rod with your right hand and the line tightly with your left hand, and that you are pointing the rod forward with about 30 feet of fly line straight out on the ground in front of you. Your left hand should be closer to your body and slightly lower than your right hand. Cast the line back—at the same time doing a *downup* with the left hand. Stop. Both hands should be back together with the rod tilting backward and the imaginary line stretched out behind you. Take your time. Now, cast the line forward with your right hand— simultaneously doing the *downup* with your left hand. Your hands should now be together in the original position in front of you with the imaginary line stretched out on the ground in front. Practice these casts until you are quite comfortable with both hands working together. Be sure to give yourself plenty of time between the backcast and the forward cast.

6.

Conclude the forward cast with both hands together, your left hand slightly below your right.

Try to false cast—at first very slowly, and then, as you develop a little rhythm, a bit faster. If you have any difficulty, revert to the separate backcast and forward cast. On the final forward cast, pull *down* with the left hand and let go. Your imaginary line will streak forward in a beautiful loop and drop gently to the water about 300 feet away.

Vary the length of the *downup* motion (and the length of the casting stroke with the right hand) using everything from a very short pull of 12 inches or so to a full extension of your arm. The lengths of the left hand pull and the right hand motion should be about the same. You may feel more comfortable holding something in your rod hand as you practice—the butt section of your fly rod, a screwdriver or even a pen or pencil. The motions will soon become second nature to you. Like riding a bicycle, it's a skill you'll never forget. I learned the double haul one morning as I was preparing to shave. I was so excited that I practiced it all day at work—in my office, on the elevator, even walking down the street. I'm sure people thought I was crazy, but that evening at the casting pools in Golden Gate Park, I succeeded in using both of my hands and cast a fly farther than I ever had before.

__Pull down and let go__ with your left hand on the imaginary final cast. Point the rod along the path of the line for a long shoot.

*Start this **double haul practice** with your hands close together in front of you and the line extended on the lawn. Overhang is the distance from the rod tip to the back end of the shooting taper. Before you begin, think through the backcast and the haul.*

Find a lawn that's at least 70 feet long. Assemble your rod and reel, and pull the shooting taper and about 30 feet of running line from the tip of the rod. Stretch the mono-filament running line for a few seconds with the help of a friend or by using a nearby tree or rock. This eliminates the coils that usually develop in monofilament wound on a reel. Take a few minutes to do the *downup* pantomime exercise again. Now pick up the rod and arrange the line so that the shooting taper and 5 to 6 feet of monofilament extend past the rod tip straight on the lawn in front of you. The length of monofilament between the tip of the rod and the beginning of the shooting taper is called the overhang. The rest of the 30 feet of monofilament running line should be in loose coils on the ground beside you. Point the rod at the fly on the ground and hold the running line tightly with your left hand. Now think this through: "I'm going to cast the line back with my right hand and go *downup* with my left hand." Take your time. Without allowing any line to slip through your left hand, backcast and stop. Your rod will be pointing backward and the shooting taper will be on the ground behind you.

Left:
The hands begin to separate as the right hand starts the backcast and the left hand initiates a downup motion.

Center:
The hands separate as the right hand makes the backcast while the left hand approaches the bottom of the downup motion.

Right:
The right hand has completed the backcast, and the left hand has bounced up to complete the downup. The hands are once again close together.

Allow the backcast to fall to the lawn behind you, and visualize what your hands must do on the forward cast.

Left:
As the right hand begins the forward stroke, the left hand simultaneously starts another downup motion. Even the body has rocked forward to begin the cast.

Center:
The left hand bounces at the bottom of the downup motion as the right hand completes the cast.

Right:
At the completion of the forward stroke and the downup, both hands are back together in front of the body. Now think through another backcast.

Think your next move through: "I'm going to cast the line forward with my right hand and go *downup* with my left hand." Once again, take plenty of time before you do it. Continue to cast the line in back and in front until you can false cast. It won't be long. Practice, using five or six false casts to develop rhythm and to continue the education of your left hand. On the final forward cast, pull with your left hand—and let go, allowing the loose line on the ground to shoot through the guides.

Be sure to use a wider casting stroke, for the combination of the heavy shooting taper and the left hand pull creates more rod bend. Generally try to cast with a heavier stroke rather than a quicker one. Remember to lead with your hand during the casting stroke and to direct the *unloading* of the rod toward the intended direction of the fly cast. This is a new and different casting experience. Be patient with yourself. A couple of hours of practice with the shooting taper and the funny hand motions will add exciting new dimensions to your casting and fishing.

After your left hand begins to function properly, work on making the following refinements: 1) Avoid jerking with the left hand. Think of both hands moving apart smoothly and at about the same rate of speed during the casting stroke. 2) False cast gently. If you false cast with too much force, the fly line bounces in the air at the end of each cast and you lose control of it. 3) If you need more line speed, let both hands and the rod drift back on the final backcast and sling the line with more power (and a harder left hand pull) on the final forward cast. Drifting the hands and rod increases the size of the casting arc to accommodate the greater rod bend on the final cast.

I recommend that you pull with your left hand *completely through the casting stroke.* That is, the left hand pull starts and ends at exactly the *same time* as the right hand casting stroke starts and ends. The start of the left hand haul helps to pull the line straight and to load the rod. The rest of the haul accelerates the line to its maximum speed.

The right hand stops (unloading the rod) at precisely the same time as the left hand bounces at the bottom of the pull. The left hand goes back up *after* the casting stroke is made and the line is on its way. Both hands also move about the *same distance* through the casting stroke. Short casting stroke equals short left hand pull; long stroke equals long pull. This full left hand pull is a very natural hand movement, and I believe you'll find it an easy and very effective technique. Practice this equal-hand movement with pantomime exercises using short and long casting strokes.

Experiment with the overhang. I find that most rods cast well with about 5 to 10 feet of overhang. Never use less than 3 to 4 feet, for the base of the shooting head will hit the rod tip. And too long an overhang results in loss of control and line speed.

Keep the backcast and forward cast in separate planes. Tilting the rod away from you on the backcast and using a vertical forward cast generally works well. On long-distance casts with shooting tapers, aim the forward cast a bit higher than usual to allow the line to carry to its maximum. Tilting the entire casting stroke back permits you to get this higher trajectory.

Try to have the running line flow through your opened left hand or form a guide by joining the tips of your thumb and middle finger (or forefinger) as you shoot line on the final forward cast. This gives you instant control when the fly hits the water and permits you to stop the cast whenever you wish. Pull out more line, then try to shoot it over the horizon.

Although you are practicing the double haul with a sinking shooting taper, this cast is equally useful with floating full lines. With a full fly line, however, the friction of the line on the guides is greater than with monofilament running line and the double haul is a bit more difficult. Once you have 35 to 40 feet (the heavy, thick portion) of a weight forward line out through the guides, the haul becomes easier. Try the double haul with your weight forward floating line. □

Left:
Hold the line tightly as you apply power to the forward cast before **shooting the line**.

Right:
Shoot the line through an O shape formed by thumb and middle finger to maintain instant control.

9

Fly Rod Drift and the Belgian Cast

Almost all good casters follow through with the fly rod after it unloads on the backcast and before they make the forward cast. They also follow through on the forward cast before they make the backcast. Essentially, this FLY ROD DRIFT is a repositioning of the rod between backcasts and forward casts—a follow-through or a reaching back (or forward) after the power stroke has been completed and before the forward (or backward) stroke begins. Drifting the rod can really help your timing between the backcast and forward cast and, at times is almost a necessity to correctly position the rod before reversing the direction of the line.

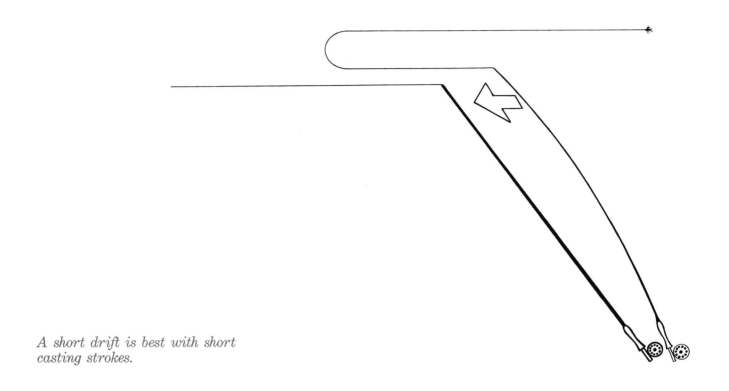

A short drift is best with short casting strokes.

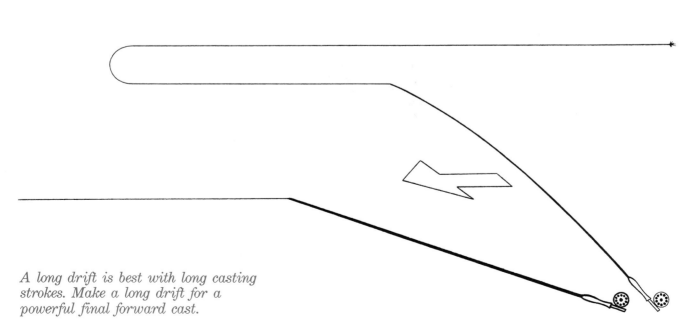

A long drift is best with long casting strokes. Make a long drift for a powerful final forward cast.

Good casters frequently increase the size of the casting arc (stroke) to accommodate any additional power and rod bend in the final forward cast. They enlarge the arc by extending (drifting) the rod back into the correct position after the backcast and just before the final forward cast. I once overheard some comments from a man watching Steve Rajeff, the current world flycasting champion, cast an entire fly line plus several yards of backing. He said something like, "Wow, what a fantastic cast! I can't believe he cast that far with just that super-short casting stroke." This onlooker was correct in that Steve did use a very narrow casting arc while gently false casting. He was also correct in not quite believing what he saw. What he hadn't noticed was the long backward drift that Steve made just before his powerful, wide arc forward cast.

One of the common faults of beginning and intermediate flycasters is a reverse drift. Most people who have have this problem make a creeping-forward motion with the rod after the backcast and just before the forward cast. This motion is the antithesis of good rod drift and usually causes a tailing loop. Creeping forward reduces the size of the casting arc on the forward cast; the shortened arc is not sufficient to accommodate the power and rod bend of the forward cast, so the loop tails. If you have the problem of a tailing or crossed casting loop, especially on long casts, drop your right foot back and watch your hand as you cast. Make sure that it is not moving forward until the backcast has almost straightened out and you're ready to make your forward cast. The best way to cure the problem, however, is to turn that fault into a virtue by learning to drift the rod in the opposite direction. Follow through.

Good rod drift is best learned without a rod and line. Practice in pantomime until you are comfortable with this follow-through motion. Drift the rod only a short distance (a very subtle follow-through) for short casts and, of course, a greater distance when you use more fly line or power.

*After the rod unloads and as the loop rolls back, **drift** back with the rod—follow through.*

The **Belgian cast** begins with a sidearm backcast.

The overhead view clearly shows the oval path of the line as it is being swung around into the forward cast.

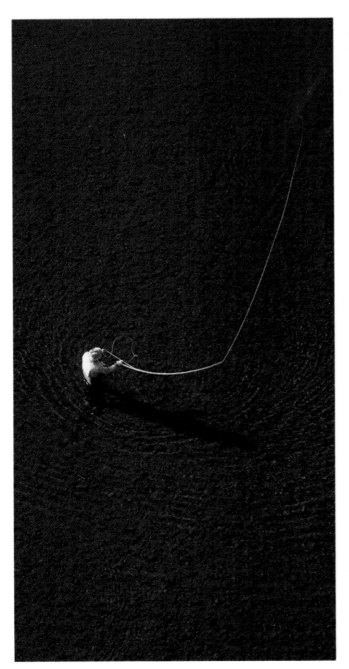

As the backcast reaches a nearly straight position, the rod has already begun the forward cast in a vertical plane.

The Belgian Cast

This interesting and useful variation of a basic flycast offers maximum control of the fly line and fly. It usually involves a wide separation of the planes of the backcast and forward cast (e.g., a sidearm backcast and an overhand forward cast), and a somewhat different rod drift between these casts. Named for its originator, Albert Godart, a world champion tournament flycaster from Belgium, the Belgian cast has variations that have been popularized in the United States by Charles Ritz, A.J. McClane, Lee Wulff, Ernest Schwiebert and others, with such descriptive titles as the oval cast, horseshoe cast, swing-around cast, wind cast and constant pressure cast. Let's consider this cast relative to other flycasts.

The basic flycast usually consists of a separate backward cast and forward cast. In the instant when the line is changing directions you momentarily lose control of the line and fly. A skilled flycaster with a fine sense of timing and good rod drift keeps that loss to a modicum. The basic flycast, with the line almost completely straight in the air—directly in line with the cast in the opposite direction—and made with the correct rod drift, is the most efficient cast under most conditions. When you're using a heavily weighted fly or a dense sinking line, however, the timing of your casts becomes critical to avoid a jarring loss of control as the line abruptly changes direction.

In the roll cast, the large loop of line behind the rod (with the end of the line in the water) serves as the backcast. The line does not reverse directions suddenly because the line in the water is basically stationary until it is pulled forward by the rolling loop. Your timing therefore need not be as precise as with the basic flycast. Although the roll cast solves many casting and fishing problems, it is not as efficient as the basic flycast made with a straight backcast in the air.

The Belgian cast usually has a slightly curved backcast somewhat similar to the rear loop in the roll cast, but in the air. Its real strength lies in its almost complete control of the fly line between the backcast and forward cast. The sideways rod drift, as you move the

*Start the **Belgian cast** with a sweeping lift into a backcast.*

Swing the line around as you raise the rod from sidearm toward vertical for the forward cast.

Deliver the forward cast in an upright plane.

rod from a sidearm backcast to an overhead forward cast, actually pulls the line through the change of direction of the fly line, and you rarely lose control of the fly and line. This added control is a big help on windy days and when you are casting large weighted flies. I use the Belgian cast often when I'm casting the faster, smaller-diameter sinking lines and shooting tapers. Another advantage of this cast is that the somewhat curved backcast, created by the wide separation of the planes of the backcast and forward cast, usually requires a little less space than a conventional straight line backcast. The shooting taper and the Belgian cast make a terrific combination when you need a long cast, but have limited backcast room. This pull-around, swing-around, constant-pressure, oval casting stroke is a winner. It's also very easy to learn.

Start with about 30 feet of fly line in front of the rod tip. Make a sidearm (horizontal) backcast and an overhead (vertical) forward cast. Backcast gently, using just enough power to get the line back into position. Swing the rod around, pulling the line into an overhead forward cast. Try to make the backcast and the forward cast one motion—a swing-around motion. Try to stay connected with the line as you change planes and directions throughout the cast. Try it with a longer line. Work with a shooting taper using both the Belgian cast and standard cast. Vary the distance between the paths of the backcast and forward cast, making narrow or wide ovals. Try it with a very short line and a narrow oval (the backcast just a foot or two to the outside of the forward cast), unloading the rod *only* on the forward cast.

I believe you'll find that you have another tool to work with in your fishing and casting and that the practice with this excellent cast will improve all of your flycasting skills. ☐

10

Presentation Casts

Flyfishing, as far as I'm concerned, is preferable to any other sort of fishing primarily because flycasting itself is so enjoyable. Some flycasters like it so much that they measure their casting skills in tournament competition, and this small group has given the flyfishing world such notable innovations as the current fly line numbering system, the double haul and the weight forward fly line. Although a few of these people consider flycasting to be an end rather than a means and delight more in the act of casting than in the fishing itself, most of the tournament casters I've known have also been dedicated fishers. For them, as for most of us, the final act required in the casting of a fly is the presentation of the fly to a fish. In that instant, the gap between flycasting and fly-fishing is suddenly bridged.

Another of the beauties of this sport is its almost limitless possibilities in fishing situations and a corresponding number of methods. Most presentation methods, however, fall within the range of a few basic techniques. These presentation casts, in addition to meeting the obvious requirements of accuracy, delicacy and distance, are simple adaptations of basic flycasting and are easy to learn. As you become more and more proficient with them, you'll find yourself adjusting to various fishing situations without a second thought. Take the time to practice these basics; they will make all the difference in your fishing.

The Straight Line Cast

The straight line cast is the easiest and probably the most commonly used presentation cast. It can be extremely accurate, and the direct connection it provides between fly and fisher offers immediate control over the fly—either for an instant retrieve or in case of an immediate strike. This direct connection permits the quick, precise control of the fly needed when float fishing for trout on a western river, tarpon and bonefish fishing on the flats, or sometimes when Atlantic salmon or steelhead fishing.

When you are fishing bugs or poppers on the surface for bass, a straight line cast enhances your chances of connecting if a bass hits your bug quickly. Both largemouth and smallmouth bass often hit a fly as soon as it lands on the water. I've even had them hit before the fly landed, actually hitting it in the air above the water, and I've missed my share of fish by throwing a cast with too much slack line. The bass has gulped, chewed and spit out the bug by the time I've gathered the slack line and tried to set the hook. At the conclusion of a straight line cast, the line and leader are both straight on the water and directly in line with the fly. The rod tip is usually down near the water and in line with the line, leader and fly.

Make this cast simply by throwing a good loop and then following the line with the rod tip to the water. Don't overpower this cast. If you do, the line will bounce back, creating the slack you want to avoid. If you need more line speed because of wind or to present the fly quickly or at a distance, use the butt cast. This wide arc casting stroke works very well for the straight line cast because it concludes with the rod tip in line with the line and leader, and the lower casting loop has a tendency to roll out straight on the water. (Review the pick up and lay down butt cast, or the Madison cast in Chapter 6, "The Application of Power.")

In float fishing, for example, you are often after trout holding along the bank, and cast toward them from a moving boat. Most strikes come right at the bank or very close to it. When the fly lands next to the bank, the straight line cast permits you to strike a fish

Left:
Useful in casting accurately to the bank, the **straight line cast** *begins with a good loop directed low over the water.*

Right:
The rod tip follows the line down to the water for immediate control over the fly.

immediately or to start a retrieve quickly. It also enables you to cover more water from the drifting boat.

One of the most impressive examples of this I've ever seen was on a float trip I took with Tom Morgan, formerly a fishing guide who now owns the Winston Rod Company in Twin Bridges, Montana. With a streamer fly cast from our drift boat, Tom used a straight line cast into the bank, ending each cast with his rod pointing right at the fly. Using what he calls a "bounce retrieve," he bounced his rod sharply several times while slowly raising his rod tip. This technique caused the fly to swim in short, abrupt darts for a few feet out from the bank. With a single backcast, Tom would then make another straight line cast into the bank in new water. This method enabled him to cover considerably more water by not having to strip or fool around with any slack line, and his straight line presentation also meant he was always ready for a hit. Combined with his unusual and very worthwhile bounce retrieve, it was devastatingly effective.

Slack Line Casts

Although the straight line cast solves many problems, it also creates a few. The worst of these is drag.

Many sorts of flyfishing with both dry and subsurface flies require a free and natural drift of the fly. Natural trout foods, and especially most insects, aren't attached to anything else in the current. Their bodies are almost weightless as they drift and turn with every subtle change of wind and water. They shimmer and shiver in or on the water in a manner that's often difficult to duplicate with a hooked imitation tied to a leader. To present such imitations successfully, you must create slack in both the leader and the fly line. I am certain that the biggest mistake made by most flyfishers in fishing a dry fly is not their choice of fly, but rather not drifting their fly naturally.

The first consideration in getting a free, natural drift is to have a leader long and light enough to present the fly with delicacy and to allow a natural float. George Harvey, for many years a renowned flyfishing professor at Penn

Straight line casts are especially useful in stillwater situations, such as bass bugging.

State, has been a strong advocate of a leader tippet light and long enough to fall on the water in a gentle series of S-shaped curves. Many contemporary leaders have tippet sections that are too short to allow this. Use at least 3 feet of tippet material to ensure adequate slack during your presentation to the fish. The Rule of Three is a good place to start when determining the proper size (thickness) of this 3-foot tippet. Divide the hook size by three for the correct tippet size (e.g., fly size 18 divided by 3 equals tippet size: 6X).

The other primary factors in achieving a good drift of your fly are both a slack line and leader. A straight, tight line on the water between your rod and the fly almost ensures failure. Every little nuance of wind and water current, plus your own rod movement, cause the fly to drag, and you lose a natural drift. You often cannot see this drag from 20 or 30 feet away, but be most assured that the trout sees it all too well. Mike Lawson of Henry's Fork Anglers in Idaho has told me that both he and his guides explain to their clients that they must try to present the fly as if it were not attached to the line. This is an excellent concept with which to introduce some slack line casts. These extremely important presentation casts are used not only with dry flies, but also with wet flies and nymphs that may require a natural, unimpaired drift.

Slack line casts are essential for most cross-stream and downstream presentations.

The Bounce Cast

Make this presentation cast so that the line and leader are fully extended while still 1 to 2 feet above the water. Use enough line speed so that when the cast stops above the water, it rebounds or "bounces" back slightly before the line, leader and fly land on the surface. That bounce creates small amounts of slack along the whole length of line and leader, especially in your long tippet section, resulting in a natural, drag-free float of the fly. You may wish to enhance the bounce by pulling back slightly on your rod or by tugging the line with your left hand as the fly line is extended over the water, particularly on a long cast. The bounce cast also offers a very delicate presentation, since the fly stops in the air and then drops gently to the water.

I often use this presentation cast in dry fly fishing (especially with the reach cast, which I describe later). After a bit of practice, you'll find that because you can control your line speed and timing, you can match the degree of bounce to a particular fishing situation. Even a novice develops this basic technique quickly; the immediate results are a better drift and more fish on the end of the line.

*Throw a slightly overpowered cast over the target to start the **bounce cast**.*

Keep the rod high to allow the line to slacken as it rebounds.

This soft bounce cast has caused moderate slack with good accuracy. A harder bounce creates more slack, but reduces accuracy.

Left:

*A good loop directed over the target starts the **wiggle cast.***

Right:

Sideways shakes of the rod put waves in the line near the rod while the top of the loop continues forward normally.

The Wiggle Cast

If the bounce cast doesn't give you enough slack, use the wiggle cast, sometimes known as the S cast because the line falls to the water in a series of gentle S curves.

After you have completed the forward casting stroke and the line loop is unrolling in the air, all you do is shake the rod. You can wiggle, jiggle, shimmy, shake, twitch or vibrate the rod any way you want. Those vibrations reverberate along the unrolling line, and it will fall to the water in a series of bends. While the intervening currents between you and the fly are straightening those bends, your fly floats without drag. You can increase or decrease the amount of slack by changing the number and the size of the wiggles. It's even possible to determine where the slack ends up in your line. Obviously, the slack is most advantageous in the fastest water between you and the fly. You can create slack at the end of the line—near the leader—by wiggling your rod early in the cast, just as the loop is forming. You can form slack in the line nearest to your rod by wiggling the rod late in the cast, after the loop is well out in front. Aim this cast and all other slack line presentation casts above the water so that the line shape gets established in the air. You may find it helpful to shoot some line through the guides while you are wiggling the rod. Shooting line largely prevents your rod wiggles from pulling the line backward and shortening your cast. Although I use the wiggle cast less often than the bounce cast or the reach cast, I still consider it an important slack line technique. Practice this cast for a short time, and you'll quickly find yourself adapting it to a variety of fishing situations.

Left:

As the tip lowers and line shoots through the guides, further wiggles of the rod put slack in the entire line.

Right:

The completed wiggle cast produces ample slack for a good, free drift of the fly.

*Make a high forward cast to initiate
the **pile cast**.*

*Lower the rod tip as the extended
line begins to fall.*

The Pile Cast

When fish are holding and rising in slow water with fast water between you and the fish, you may need another slack line variation called the pile cast. Use this cast when you want an extreme amount of slack near the fly.

All you have to do is aim your forward cast higher than normal—almost as if you're casting toward the horizon or treetops. As the unrolling line travels skyward, lower your rod tip toward the water. As the back of the line falls, the front end of the line and the leader collapse, landing in a wonderful pile of slack. During the resultant perfect drift, Moby Trout will inhale the fly and you'll have another perfect day astream. Once again, it's an easy technique to learn, it's fun to do, and it will occasionally enable you to take a fish that you otherwise would miss.

The end of the line and the leader fall limply in a pile of slack.

Slack concentrated near the fly and fish produces a drag-free drift on this downstream cast.

The Fly First Cast

This extremely accurate cast is most often used for pocket water fishing. It's an excellent way to fish those small hot spots in broken fast water. The fly touches down on the water before the line or leader in an almost perfect presentation, and the extra moment of natural drift before the line falls and is swept away by the current is often all that it takes to attract fast-reacting fish. I have a special feeling about this presentation cast. Jack Horner, one of my mentors in flycasting and a genuine legend in western trout fishing, used it extensively and considered it a sign of a good caster. The cast can be extremely effective at times, and target shooting on the river is fun.

Make this cast by simply throwing a high backcast and then overpowering an overhead (vertical) forward cast. The extra power drives the fly and leader down past the straight fly line, allowing the fly to alight on the water an instant before the line drops. Aim the cast a foot or two above the water and stop the rod high. After the fly dips to the water, drop the tip of your rod and point it at the fly. This extra slack doubles the free drift time of your fly. Use short, strong tippets and short casts. Remember, the key to this cast is to stop the rod high and direct the loop down.

Left:

*For the **fly first presentation,** the rod tip stops high, angling the line down toward the target. A high backcast allows the forward cast to be directed downward.*

Right:

The stopped rod tip checks the line, and the impetus of the cast causes the fly to flick downward to alight before leader and line.

The **reach cast** begins with a
normal forward cast.

As the loop extends, reach the rod to
the side, allowing line to slide
through the guides to avoid pulling
the fly off target.

By positioning the back of the line, the reach cast presents the fly to the fish at a better angle.

Left:
*Begin the **reach cast curve** with a sideward reach during the forward cast.*

Right:
Return the rod to the straightaway position while the line is still in the air to form the curve in the line.

The Reach Cast

Of all the slack line presentations I've described, this cast, first popularized by Doug Swisher and Carl Richards, is my favorite. One of the most versatile casts in trout fishing, the reach cast is also easy to do. This presentation cast consists of moving the back end of the fly line to either the right or left side of the caster during the cast, usually upstream. All you have to do is make your normal forward cast toward the target and, while the line unrolls in the air, reach with your rod to the right or left. The fly will land where you want it, but instead of landing straight between you and the target, the back end of the line (closest to you) will be moved dramatically. When you make the reach, let some line slide through the guides to avoid pulling the fly off target.

I use this cast often when fishing across and downstream and where fast currents run between me and the fish. With this cast, an upstream reach effectively creates a large curve of slack line that gets dragged by the faster current long before the fly's drift is affected. Just as important, this cast presents the fly to the fish at a good angle. For example, when you are fishing across and downstream, an up-stream reach cast causes a gentle curve of line, leader and fly to bow upstream of the fish. The fly drifts to the fish without dragging and ahead of either the leader or line—an ideal situation. Reaching early or late in the casting stroke results in a curve either closer to the fly or to the caster (as in the wiggle cast).

An excellent variation of this cast is the reach cast curve. While the line is still in the air and after you've made a reach, return your rod to the straightaway position. Now when the line falls on the water, it will have a broad curve in it to the right or left, depending on the direction of your reach. This could well be called "mending the line in the air," since you are adjusting the line to the current's speed before the line hits the water instead of afterward. The reach cast curve is the most accurate and dependable curve cast you can use with the long, extremely delicate tippets that are popular in much of trout fishing today.

*The **positive curve cast** starts with a sidearm cast and horizontal loop.*

The impetus of the cast kicks the fly and leader across to the caster's left.

Line, leader and fly settle to the water in a decided curve to the left. The same cast made from an off-shoulder position produces a curve to the right.

Positive Curve Cast

When you use shorter or stronger tippets or heavier flies, the positive curve cast handles the situation well. This cast is identical to the fly first presentation, except that it is horizontal rather than vertical. Start by tilting the rod away from you, then simply overpower the cast. The extra force with the angled or horizontal loop kicks the leader and fly past the straight fly line into a curve on the opposite side of the tilted rod (i.e., a right-hand tilt causes a left-hand curve, while canting the rod over the left shoulder drives the fly into a right-hand curve).

Negative Curve Cast

A negative curve cast can be made by using the same horizontal casting loop as with the positive curve cast and *underpowering* the cast so that the line collapses on the water before it straightens out. Thus, a right-hand tilt causes a curve to the right. This negative curve cast works best with long delicate tippets and light flies. I find this cast hard to control and rarely use it.

Striking the Fish

Striking the fish while you have slack line on the water presents few problems, not only because of the very long movement that's possible with a fly rod, but also because of the friction of the thick fly line against the water. Angling writers frequently recommend a sideways strike with the rod tip close to the water. I must admit, however, that most of the time I instinctively raise the rod on the strike, and it seems to make very little, if any, difference. The key to striking a fish on a slack line presentation (or in almost all fishing situations) is to be sure you have no slack between your rod tip and the water. A good general rule is to keep your rod tip close to the water and pointed toward the fly at all times.

One key word for learning these and a myriad of other possible presentation and fishing techniques is *experiment*. As you begin to understand and apply these basic techniques, flyfishing will become both easier and more enjoyable. And, not least of all the consequences, you'll catch more fish.

Conclusion

I started this book by telling you that rolling a loop of line back and forth in the air is fun. I will conclude by suggesting that, for me, flyfishing without flycasting is incomplete. Together they often add up to something more than their parts.

I must tell you of a special evening on an Argentine river in Tierra del Fuego. The Río Grande meanders through a treeless, windswept tundra, and although it holds a good run of sea-run brown trout, reveals little beauty or character in its even flow. Despite a week of windy cold weather and spotty fishing, I developed an attachment for this lonely river and its giant moody sky. On the last evening of my stay, I left my friends and hiked a short distance upriver, arriving at my favorite pool less than an hour before dark. Starting at the top in knee-deep water, I worked downstream casting the 70 feet or so to the opposite bank. The wind, that had been blowing hard, stopped. The sky started to light up with the sunset, and for a moment I considered wading back and climbing a small hill to photograph the sky and water. "Just another picture of a sunset—the usual photographic cliche," I rationalized, "The hell with it. I'll fish." I soon worked into a comfortable rhythm—cast, mend, swing the fly, step downstream and cast again. The fly began to drop perfectly in the small openings in the irregular bank. Casting effortlessly, I felt I could practically will the fly to the distant targets. Orange light moved over the barren hills and flickered on the moving water. The colors deepened and the magic of the casting and the hour became even more intense. Exultant and feeling completely alone, I started to sing loud snatches of songs, unthinking and a bit wild as I fished through the pool. I knew that I did not want a fish to disturb my fishing. □